T0357344

estherpress

Books for Courageous Women

ESTHER PRESS VISION

Publishing diverse voices that encourage and equip women to walk courageously in the light of God's truth for such a time as this.

BIBLICAL STATEMENT OF PURPOSE

"For if you keep silent at this time, relief and deliverance will rise for the Jews from another place, but you and your father's house will perish. And who knows whether you have not come to the kingdom for such a time as this?"

Esther 4:14 (ESV)

What people are saying about …

YOU'RE NOT TOO LATE

"Have you ever asked yourself, *Why does it seem like everyone else is getting what I deeply desire for myself?* If so, this book is for you. *You're Not Too Late* is a beautifully crafted reminder that the pace of our lives is not dictated by the world but by the divine timing of God. With raw honesty and vulnerability, Rebecca explores the universal struggle of feeling behind and then offers steps to trust God's plan for your life. Grounded in solid biblical principles, this book is a must-read for anyone who has ever questioned their path, reminding us that with God, we are always right on time."

Jennifer Dukes Lee, author of *Growing Slow* and *It's All Under Control*

"Reading a book by Rebecca is like a reassuring conversation with a friend who knows exactly how it feels to struggle with the disappointments of life and wonder if it's too late to hope again. It's not just a book to read; it's a journey to letting go of doubt and fear, trusting in God's plan, and embracing the truth that you're never too late for His love and purpose. It's a lifeline for anyone struggling with the pressures of life's timeline, offering hope, biblical insight, strength, and a renewed sense of purpose. If you're seeking to trust God's timing and find peace in His promises, *You're Not Too Late* is an absolute must-read."

Tammy Trent, author, speaker, singer, cohost Life Today TV

"Rebecca has a unique way of making you feel safe and seen, which prepares your heart for what the Lord wants you to receive through her writing. Most of us spend a good portion of our lives holding the tension between patiently seeking God's will and the worldly clock that ticks loudly around us. *You're Not Too Late* invites you to dismantle and discard what is holding you back while propelling you into the arms of the One who holds the future. Through Rebecca's transparency with her own personal journey, this book lays out practical life applications to explore where God's presence can be found in your struggle. It also helps reveal faulty narratives that need to be surrendered to move forward, pointing us back to the truth that He is truly working all things for the good of those who love and seek Him."

Dina Deleasa Gonsar, author of *At the Kitchen Sink*, speaker, and television personality

"As someone who listens to, meets with, and counsels many women, I can attest to the relevance and wisdom this book provides. The transparency in which Rebecca connects her personal journey to the truth of Scripture and the trustworthiness of God will serve as an encouragement to readers, whether new believers or seasoned saints! I am particularly grateful for the practical way Rebecca leads readers through questions of personal reflection that get to the heart of issues we face in learning to trust God and his timing. One thing is certain, our hurry-up world isn't slowing down anytime soon. This book tosses a lifeline to those desiring rest in the Lord and the peace that comes in service to a trustworthy God."

Tasha Calvert, author, Bible teacher, host of *Digging In* podcast, and women's ministry director of Prestonwood Church

"Rebecca's message is one that resonates with so many women today. It's a reminder that no matter where you are in life, God has placed you there for a reason. This book encourages you to take a breath, embrace your present, and trust that there's a bigger plan at work—one that's often beyond what you can see right now. It's about finding joy in the present moment instead of stressing about what comes next."

Hope Reagan Harris, founder of Purpose Doesn't Pause, author of *Purpose Doesn't Pause* and *This Is My Happy Place*, podcaster, and friend

"Rebecca knows what it is to wait. How it feels to watch friend after friend get the thing you've been praying for. How it hurts to wrestle with your attitude and with God's timing. Reading *You're Not Too Late* feels like sitting down to coffee with a trusted friend: you open your heart and your Bible, invite God to join the conversation, and go home smiling and changed. Packed with inspiring personal stories and applications for women in all ages and stages of life, *You're Not Too Late* is part rich Bible study, part practical workbook, and all good for the soul.

Elizabeth Laing Thompson, author of numerous books for women and teens including *When God Says, "Wait,"* and *All the Feels*

AN INTERACTIVE BOOK
WITH TEN SESSIONS
OF VIDEO INCLUDED

Rebecca George

YOU'RE NOT TOO LATE

Trusting God's Timing in a Hurry-Up World

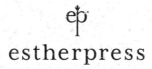

estherpress

Books for Courageous Women
from David C Cook

YOU'RE NOT TOO LATE
Published by Esther Press,
an imprint of David C Cook
4050 Lee Vance Drive
Colorado Springs, CO 80918 U.S.A.

Integrity Music Limited, a Division of David C Cook
Brighton, East Sussex BN1 2RE, England

Esther Press®, the EP logo, DAVID C COOK® and related marks are registered trademarks of David C Cook.

All rights reserved. Except for brief excerpts for review purposes,
no part of this book may be reproduced or used in any form
without written permission from the publisher.

The website addresses recommended throughout this book are offered as a resource
to you. These websites are not intended in any way to be or imply an endorsement
on the part of David C Cook, nor do we vouch for their content.

All Scripture quotations are taken from the ESV® Bible (The Holy Bible, English Standard Version®), copyright
© 2001 by Crossway, a publishing ministry of Good News Publishers. Used by permission. All rights reserved.

Library of Congress Control Number 2024943979
ISBN 978-0-8307-8437-0
eISBN 978-0-8307-8438-7

© 2025 Rebecca George

The Team: Susan McPherson, Julie Cantrell, Judy Gillispie, Kristen Defevers, James Hershberger, Susan Murdock
Cover Design: Brian Mellema

Printed in the United States of America
First Edition 2025

1 2 3 4 5 6 7 8 9 10

010325

To Dustin

By God's provision alone, you are the redemptive character in this book. I'll never get over how he answered our prayers for each other. I know more of God's holiness, goodness, and grace because I've walked alongside you. You are my husband who also happens to be my pastor. I hope that's evident as you read these pages. Thank you for shepherding me to God's throne. I love you the most I ever have and the least I ever will.

CONTENTS

INTRODUCTION

Every chapter of our lives will be marked by longing. There's simply no way around it until we reach heaven. How much time do we spend waiting? Waiting for more, for less, for different, for better. Can I let you in on a secret? *You're not too late for your life.* I know we're new friends here, but I'm positive that this much is true: my heart *aches*, and so does yours. It aches over all manner of disappointment, regret, and unfulfilled desire.

I know it's true because you and I are living between two Edens. God created mankind to live in perfect fellowship with him in the garden of Eden (Gen. 1–3). After the fall, when sin entered the picture, we began to see and experience the effects of a broken world. It seems, with each passing day, we hear more and more evidence that the world is turning toward sin and self as a means to satisfy (Rom. 1). However, there is great hope that—although we find ourselves bumping into brokenness at every turn—one day we will experience perfect fellowship with God when he restores all things and eliminates all sin, pain, and grief with finality (Rev. 21). "How do we make sense of the in-between?" is the question likely lingering in your heart. This book is my attempt to wrestle with that very tension using Scripture as my compass.

There are a few reasons this book might be enticing to you. Maybe you feel trapped in the common struggles that emerge when it seems like you're too late in a *hurry-up world*. You likely find yourself grappling with cynicism, idolatry, disappointment, or regret. You desire to turn toward the Father in trust but often find yourself slipping back into old patterns of thinking. Perhaps you're at the end of yourself, fatigued from disappointing circumstances, seemingly impossible scenarios, or the tight grip you hold on your unrealistic expectations.

Maybe you're the type of reader who needs confirmation that an author has the chops to speak into the deepest recesses of your heart. *I understand.* Your heart, with the hurt and disappointment it carries, is precious and sensitive. You and I both should see it as the Father sees it: *valuable* and *sacred.* Can I offer you a few bullet points from my résumé of longing as a comfort that we're in this together?

- I wore *twelve* dresses that were **not** white down the aisles of friends' weddings before I became a *bride.*
- I've been passed up for promotions in my corporate career that I felt I deserved.
- My husband, Dustin, was forty-four years old when he proposed to me, and we both spent many years wondering if God would ever fulfill what we felt was his desire for us both to be married. Dustin was also a single lead pastor for many years (a reality that often comes with a lot of opinions and rejection).
- I've watched and walked with dear friends through the horrors that come along with infertility and hoping to be called *Mom.*

- I've spent years of a career in corporate America desiring to write and speak in full-time ministry.
- I've watched my mom walk through cancer and interceded for her in the "meanwhile" between *test* and *result*, wondering if God would answer our prayer in the way we hoped.

Longing comes in different forms and is no respecter of persons. No one escapes its grip; somehow there's at least a little bit in each of us. It has marked my life at every turn, and I've struggled to understand the fine line between my earthly desires and God's will. Because you hold these words in your hand, I bet you have too. From the outset, I want to make you a couple of promises.

First, I promise to press hard against the urge to tie your heart's desires into a neat bow. This would be incredibly unkind of me as an author. It's natural, particularly if you're an optimist, to take the desires we feel and spin them into something positive. We must anchor our hearts in truth that we can hang our hats on, but you will not find toxic positivity, comfy platitudes, or empty promises inside these pages.

Second, I promise that I will point you in the direction of the gospel at every turn. Practices and strategies are good (and I'll share many), but what our aching hearts need is to better understand the redemption story God has written across the pages of Scripture that now intersects with our lives. The world doesn't need another book that offers suggestions for better living. We need a new narrative for how we think about the areas of life where we feel *too late*.

This message chronicles my own journey of struggle and triumph as I've had to look up at Jesus, unsure of the outcome, and press forward in

dependence on his wisdom and strength with my hands open in surrender to his better plan. I am in this with you, and with everything in me I want us to walk away knowing God's heart for our longing more deeply.

THROUGHOUT THE BOOK

- Each of the ten chapters will explore common challenges we will face as we learn to trust God's timing. I'll share stories of personal struggles in these areas and explore how to turn toward Scripture as our foundation.
- The end-of-chapter activities will walk you through how to turn from unhelpful thought patterns and behaviors toward thoughts and behaviors that are more in line with Scripture.
- We will explore case studies to see how each chapter's particular struggle might play out in a relational or vocational longing.
- You'll also find an accompanying video for each chapter in which I will guide you through specific action steps. This video content is free to you and can be viewed alone or with a group. Access the videos by visiting the link or scanning the QR code at the end of this chapter.

This book is for the hopefuls, the almost-but-not-yets, the crushed in defeat, the stunned by a lack of progress, and the weary woman ready to hang up her jersey. This is for the girl who snuck away during her best friend's wedding reception because she couldn't choke back tears any longer over her desire to be the one in white. This is for the woman whose lived experience doesn't line up with cultural norms (and she feels *less than* because of the waiting). This is for the prayerful wife who can't bear to see one line across a pregnancy test … One. More. Time. This is for the gal who feels looked over or picked last. Your tears are not in vain. He sees every single one (Ps. 56:8) and is well acquainted with your grief (Isa. 53:3).

There will always be a low hum in our culture whispering, *Then you'll be happy.* The answer to your pain is not to sit on your hands, awaiting the moment when God will orchestrate your wildest dreams. No, there is a great purpose exactly where he has placed your feet *right now.* I know you're struggling to cling to that truth today. If I'm honest, there are many days when I'm in the fight with you.

You are not too late. We're on God's watch, and it *is possible* to open our hands in surrender as we lay our desires in his trustworthy arms. He sees the entirety of our lives from the perspective of eternity.

These pages are for you, my dear friend.

Access the Videos Here:
https://davidccook.org/access
Access Code: NotTooLate
Or scan this QR code:

Chapter 1

DESPAIR & JOY

"You want to go for a hike?" my friend Sara texted as we both wrapped up an exhausting week at work. I'd grown up in the foothills of the Great Smoky Mountains, and I had come to savor the beauty and splendor of East Tennessee, so a hiking day with Sara sounded perfect.

"Sure," I replied, encouraged to know that, at least for a while, I could forget about what had been plaguing my heart so deeply: *singleness*. Hiking has always done that for me. My mind has never been able to focus on both where I'll place my foot next *and* the troubles of life.

The next day, Sara picked me up in her Honda Pilot. With the windows rolled down, we drove down the curvy roads that led to the trailhead. When I stepped out, I took a slow, deep breath of mountain air, and we began walking inside the national park. My feet pressed into the trail, and we made our way across gravel, mud, leaves, and a few streams as we adventured along Middle Prong Trail.

I'd been hiking plenty of times in the Smokies—Rainbow Falls, the Chimney Tops, Clingmans Dome—but I'd never walked this trail. The more we walked, the more special it began to feel, although I wasn't sure why. My heart couldn't possibly have known what God was orchestrating.

Sara was trudging through a difficult season at the time, and I … well, I just wanted to find my husband and get married. Sara and I both brought immense pain and frustration to the hike that day, and we both needed the sound of the stream and the trail beneath our feet. We talked a little, but through a good bit of the hike I prayed silently:

God, it seems everywhere I turn, everyone around me is experiencing the life I desire to have. You created marriage for a reason, and I know you have given me the desire to share my life with someone. Please show me where my longings don't align with your plan for my life. Help me turn to you in trust when I want to HURRY to the next phase. I beg you to give me patience, God, and remind me I'm NOT TOO LATE. I'm right where you want me to be.

That day, and for many days that followed, my heart couldn't process why life wasn't "happening" for me the way I wanted. I was so weary of waiting. I bet you've felt that tension too.

What I didn't know was that God was already putting his plan into place.

Early in the day, Sara and I had stopped at a bench that overlooked the most beautiful waterfall. Because it was late in the summer, the forest was bursting with bright green leaves of every size and shape. As we took a break on the bench and enjoyed the view, another hiker offered to snap a picture of us. Although it was a seemingly mundane moment on a sweltering day, years later I would learn just how significant that bench would become in my own story of trusting God's timing in a hurry-up world.

RELATIONAL AND VOCATIONAL LONGING

While hiking the trail, Sara and I were each battling our own unique longings and wrestling with God. Little did we realize, he was with us every step of the way—hearing us, seeing us, and leading us to exactly where we both needed to be.

While everyone's challenges will look different at each life phase, in this book I'll walk with you through ten main areas of struggle. We can think of these areas in two categories:

> A **relational longing** might look like a desire to be married, have children, or reconcile a relationship.

> A **vocational longing** might look like a desire to move into a new position in your job, start a business, or transition into a new season in your career.

Perhaps you're facing a prolonged season of waiting in multiple areas, and life isn't going as you'd hoped. In each chapter, we'll not only process our longings, but we'll also tear apart the false beliefs the world tells us and discover how God's Word counters those lies with truth.

Let's begin by considering the way we define *joy*.

> The world tells us: **My joy depends on my longing coming to fruition.**

> God tells us: **Biblical joy only comes from abiding in Jesus.**

As Christians, our joy should be an outward expression of our inward relationship with God. But, sometimes, the Enemy tricks us into believing that God is playing some sort of cosmic game with us. We may start to buy into the world's lie and think that we need to check the right boxes, do the right things, lose enough weight, work hard enough, and so on. Then, and only then, we may tip the scales enough to earn God's favor and finally get what we really want in life.

Do any of these examples sound familiar to you?

Maybe if I try harder …
Maybe if I show up earlier than anyone else …
Maybe if I research potential solutions a little longer …
Maybe if I dress cuter …
Maybe if I lower my expectations …
Maybe if I compromise in this particular area of conviction …
Maybe if I lose weight …
Maybe if I wake up earlier …
Maybe if I join THAT dating app …

When I think about turning from despair to joy, the psalmist's words in Psalm 126:5–6 come to mind: "Those who sow in tears shall reap with shouts of joy! He who goes out weeping, bearing the seed for sowing, shall come home with shouts of joy, bringing his sheaves with him."

CHASING THE NEXT THING, ALBEIT A WORTHY PURSUIT MANY TIMES, WILL NEVER RESULT IN LASTING CONTENTMENT OR SATISFACTION. IT WILL ONLY LEAVE US WANTING MORE OF WHAT THE WORLD HAS TO OFFER.

As followers of Christ, our present pain has an expiration date: when Jesus returns or calls us home. We will often go out into the field weary, carrying both our tears and the seeds we sow. But one day, here or in heaven, we'll experience a redemptive harvest.

Chasing the next thing, albeit a worthy pursuit many times, will never result in lasting contentment or satisfaction. It will only leave us wanting more of what the world has to offer. If we sow to the flesh, focusing on things that will not matter in eternity, we will reap the things of the flesh. If we sow in the Spirit, fixing our eyes on eternal things that will last, we will reap eternal life (Gal. 6:8–10). And yet, I wonder if any of these behavior patterns sound familiar to you?

> **Friendship:** Placing our joy in the hands of an imperfect person.

> **Marriage:** Expecting our spouse to satisfy our heart in a way that only God can.

> **Career:** Chasing after the next rung on the corporate ladder.

> **Motherhood:** Putting all our energy, focus, and concern toward our children, oftentimes at the expense of our relationship with Jesus. Our joy will rise and fall to the beat of their positive and negative behaviors.

> **Hobbies:** Learning a new hobby as a temporary distraction from our desires.

Much like trying to fill a pot with a hole in the bottom, we often pour our time, resources, and energy into activities or people that can only bring us temporary happiness. Eventually, all the water will drain out of our pots and leave us feeling empty again. Why? Because nothing in this world can offer lasting joy.

The good news? We don't have to EARN the reward of experiencing true JOY. It's a free gift we receive as we abide in Jesus.

As we learn to trust in God's timing, we'll rely on three key elements to help us find joy in the waiting.

> **The Word:** By reading Scripture, we learn more about God and what his story of redemption means for our lives today. We cannot move from despair to joy without rooting ourselves in Scripture.

> **God's character:** His ways are always consistent with his character. The more we seek him, the more we understand his limitless love for us.

> **God's presence:** He is present *everywhere* and *all the time.* We carry the Holy Spirit within us wherever we go. Therefore, we are never alone—even when we walk through seasons of hardship.

Jesus told us that the Enemy comes to steal, kill, and destroy (see John 10:10). The Enemy would love nothing more than for us to become distracted by despair and disappointment. Satan wants to prevent us from hoping in how God will show up and work in our lives.

To see our situation through a different lens, we have to choose to replace the world's lies with God's truth as it's shown to us in Romans 8:28: "And we know that for those who love God all things work together for good, for those who are called according to his purpose."

Ask yourself:

Will I focus on my despair?
Or will I fix my eyes on Jesus amid my despair?

Does this mean we have no role to play in God's purposes for us? Far from it.

In fact, despair can be a gift. It leaves us with nowhere to look but up at Jesus, the only one who will ever bring lasting joy (2 Cor. 4:18).

HE CAN HANDLE YOUR DESPAIR

I love that I grew up in the South. There's nothing I'd rather listen to than '90s country music, no place I'd rather be than Dollywood, and no beverage I'd rather be sippin' than peach tea on my Mamaw's back porch while I snap beans. However, growing up in a traditional southern culture came with a handful of behaviors that I'm not sure have served me all that well: the chief of which is shoving things under the rug.

What do I mean by that?

When I first married Dustin, we quickly realized that we have very different communication styles. (Isn't this the case in any marriage?)

His: Direct and plainly spoken.

Mine: Well,… anything but that.

After a few years of marriage, we've learned to appreciate these differences. But in the early days, he would be quick to raise an issue and work through it while I would ruminate for days, afraid I would hurt his feelings.

Maybe an example would help.

I married Dustin in May 2019, and after our honeymoon, I moved to Mississippi with him—eight hours away from my family in Tennessee. In the months that followed, I longed to go home, but I also didn't want to run from this new season of life. After a couple of months, I was still learning how to express my wants and needs. So after many days of wondering how Dustin would respond, I finally said, with some trepidation, "Hey, babe, would you mind if I went to visit my family?"

Dustin peered at me with a confused expression and said, "Sure! I think that's a great idea!"

Relief filled my heart!

Many years later, after a lot of practice, I've become more confident in expressing what I need. Maybe you're nothing like me, and these types of conversations have always come naturally to you. For those of us who share this struggle, we can take this opportunity to search our hearts and ask, *Do I do the same thing with God?*

It's easy to relate to our heavenly Father in the same way we navigate our earthly relationships. I am encouraged by the words of King David, a man after God's own heart, who grieved his pain and asked God hard questions.

Let's take a closer look at how David cried out to God in the following psalms. Underline or highlight words that resonate with you as we turn to Scripture to answer our heart's most tender questions.

Can I really be honest with God about how exhausted I am?

> I am weary with my moaning;
>> every night I flood my bed with tears;
>> I drench my couch with my weeping.
> My eye wastes away because of grief;
>> it grows weak because of all my foes. (Ps. 6:6–7)

Has God forgotten about me?

> How long, O LORD? Will you forget me forever?
>> How long will you hide your face from me?
> How long must I take counsel in my soul
>> and have sorrow in my heart all the day? (Ps. 13:1–2)

Will God ever answer my prayer?

> My God, my God, why have you forsaken me?
>> Why are you so far from saving me, from the words of
>>> my groaning?
> O my God, I cry by day, but you do not answer,
>> and by night, but I find no rest. (Ps. 22:1–2)

Does God really see, or care about, my longings?

> O Lord, all my longing is before you;
>> my sighing is not hidden from you. (Ps. 38:9)

Am I running out of time?

> O LORD, make me know my end
>   and what is the measure of my days;
>   let me know how fleeting I am!
> Behold, you have made my days a few handbreadths,
>   and my lifetime is as nothing before you.
>   Surely all mankind stands as a mere breath!
>   (Ps. 39:4–5)

Does God really see my hidden sin?

> For I know my transgressions,
>   and my sin is ever before me.
> Against you, you only, have I sinned
>   and done what is evil in your sight,
> so that you may be justified in your words
>   and blameless in your judgment. (Ps. 51:3–4)

Does God notice my weariness?

> Hear my cry, O God,
>   listen to my prayer;
> from the end of the earth I call to you
>   when my heart is faint.
> Lead me to the rock
>   that is higher than I. (Ps. 61:1–2)

Can I really take heart that I will experience the comfort of God?

> Answer me, O LORD, for your steadfast love is good;
>> according to your abundant mercy, turn to me.
> Hide not your face from your servant,
>> for I am in distress; make haste to answer me.
>>> (Ps. 69:16–17)

God isn't indifferent toward our despair, nor does he turn his ear away from our heart's cry. We cannot hide from him. He sees our every action, knows our every thought, and is jealous for our affection.

His arms are a safe place for your despair to land. There is no need to fear intimacy with him. His presence is where we experience fullness of joy here on earth (Ps. 16:11).

> THE GOOD NEWS? WE DON'T HAVE TO _EARN_ THE REWARD OF EXPERIENCING TRUE _JOY._ IT'S A FREE GIFT WE RECEIVE AS WE ABIDE IN JESUS.

DON'T NAME IT AND CLAIM IT

When I decided to write a book about trusting God's timing, I could have included empty promises, focusing on what I hope God will bring to your life if you'll only trust him, have enough faith, or pray *just a little* harder. Instead, I've chosen to wrestle with the sometimes-hard-to-understand truths we find in Scripture. We face danger as followers of Christ when we are unwilling to sit in the messy middle between our desire and the outcome.

A trend has slowly emerged that sounds appealing to our ears. It's easy to let this false narrative seep into our hearts and believe that if we can *wish* it, *speak* it, *dream* it, *pray* it, *seek* it, *name* it, or *claim* it, then it's ours for the taking. This *is* the prosperity gospel. This equation, when worked out to its logical end, leads us to destructive thinking.

The prosperity gospel says:	My Faith + My Human Effort = My Desired Result
Historic Christianity says:	My Weakness + His Strength = His Best Plan for Me

God never promised that we'll receive everything we desire. Nor did he tell us that all our dreams will be met in the way we wish. Temporarily, it would *feel* better to our aching hearts to believe that if we muster up enough human effort and courage, God will give us what we want. However, in doing so, we would be neglecting the truth that our sovereign God is the orchestrator of life. Remember, his ways and thoughts are higher than ours (see Isa. 55:8–9).

Psalm 37:4 shows us that God will give us the desires of our hearts, but we can't overlook the beginning of this verse, which says the desires of our hearts are found by *delighting in him*. If we really want to discover true joy, we must always have our eyes on him in complete and total reliance.

By now, you might be thinking, *Okay, I get it. A real relationship with Jesus equals joy. But how would this look in my everyday life?*

I'm so glad you asked.

"SEARCH ME, GOD!" PRAYER

I have been walking with Jesus since my parents led me to Christ on Easter Sunday when I was ten years old. I was raised in the church, and, having read my Bible for more than two decades, there are passages of Scripture that have seeped their way deep into my heart. Psalm 139:23–24 is one of those passages for me.

In this psalm, David prayed and praised God for his knowledge and presence in our lives. He recognized that God knew his thoughts, his path, and his sleep and that God was always with him. David acknowledged that God was trustworthy to examine his heart. The same goes for us today.

Search me, O God, and know my heart!
Try me and know my thoughts!
And see if there be any grievous way in me,
and lead me in the way everlasting!
(Psalm 139:23–24)

Throughout this book, we will rely on Psalm 139 as a compass to direct our prayers and invite God to examine our hearts. To help us focus, we'll split this passage into four prompts:

Recognize my thoughts: We'll ask God to show us our anxious thoughts.	
Reveal my sin: We'll ask God to reveal our sin while honoring Jesus' great sacrifice.	
Realign my attitude: We'll ask God to realign our thoughts to his will.	
Remember God's way: We'll ask God to impart his wisdom as we walk in his ways.	

I pray this framework helps you express your heart to God. Joy comes on the other side of our abiding delight in the God who numbers days, hairs, and seasons—not when our days turn out exactly as we planned (1 Chron. 28:9; Job 12:10; Matt. 10:26–31). His presence and infinite knowledge are close comforts when our despair feels all-consuming.

Consider the following questions:

Recognize my thoughts: What is causing my despair during this season of my life?	
Reveal my sin: Is there a sin pattern (in word or deed) that has caused my despair?	

Realign my attitude: How does my attitude need to change so I can experience true joy even in my waiting?	
Remember God's way: What is my next step as I aim to experience joy in him?	

CASE STUDY

We all feel despair at times, even though our specific situations may differ greatly. At each chapter's end, you'll find a case study that can help you relate the chapter's content to your own story, provide context for group discussion, and give encouragement as you take next steps. It's my hope that these examples will also help us develop empathy for those who may be facing different circumstances.

❀ MEET LAURA

Laura, a real estate agent in her forties, believes in the beauty of God's design for marriage and family. Her story hasn't turned out the way she'd hoped, and she has grappled with loneliness and unfulfilled desires. Despite those struggles, she discovered joy in Christ.

CHALLENGES

Unfulfilled Desires: Laura always envisioned herself as a wife and mother by this stage of life. The reality of being single challenged her dreams and triggered feelings of inadequacy.

Social Pressures: She often felt like she was falling short of societal expectations (particularly within her church community); well-intentioned questions and comments about her relationship status became increasingly common.

Isolation: She experienced deep disappointment as she watched friends and acquaintances enter new seasons of life that she hadn't experienced yet. She felt left out and looked over.

JOURNEY TO JOY

Laura began to see her singleness as an opportunity rather than being embarrassed or let down by her relationship status. She didn't shove away her desire to find a partner, but in this season of longing, she committed to seeking God's purposes for her life. Laura kept herself close to the church and built relationships with a small group of women who were walking through a similar life phase. Together, they found encouragement in what God was doing.

Between showing houses and closing deals as a real estate agent, Laura began pursuing activities that aligned with her gifts. She auditioned for a local theater's production of her favorite Broadway show, served in her local church's children's ministry, and took a painting class. She began to see her singleness as a blessing that allowed her the capacity to enjoy hobbies she might not have had time for if she were married or raising a family.

More importantly, as she continued to study Scripture with her small group and in her personal time with the Lord, she was learning to find joy in Christ rather than in a relationship. While she still hopes that God will one day provide a spouse for her to share her life with, she's no longer *waiting on marriage* to live her life. She now realizes that joy in Christ isn't saved for an exclusive set of circumstances. It's available to her (and YOU) for the taking TODAY!

Even in this season, Laura now trusts that God isn't ignoring her desires, nor does he want her to mask her struggles. She's embracing the season she's in, knowing God has meaningful plans for her life.

CASE STUDY REFLECTION PROMPTS

1. In what way do you relate to Laura's story?

2. What could you do this week to move from despair to joy?

SCRIPTURE FOR REFLECTION

- Matthew 10:26–31
- Hebrews 12:2
- Galatians 6:8–10
- Psalm 126
- John 10:10

QUESTIONS FOR REFLECTION

1. In what areas of your own life do you feel disappointment?

2. Do you ever feel like your despair is too much for God?

3. What does it mean to have joy in Christ (even in a season of hardship or suffering)?

4. How do you sense God wants you to shift your thoughts and actions to move toward joy?

5. Read the following psalms, and note how they encourage you to bring your despair to God. See Psalms 6:6–7; 12:1–2; 22:1–2; and 38:4–9.

Chapter 2

IDOLATRY & SURRENDER

A few years ago, I was invited to speak at a women's retreat hosted at a bed-and-breakfast in Tennessee. My jaw dropped when I visited Blue Mountain Mist for the first time. Although just a couple miles from Dollywood and a hop, skip, and a jump from the tourist hub of Gatlinburg, this retreat venue was tucked away in the breathtaking hollers of East Tennessee.

Apart from scheduled fellowship, sessions, and meals, I was given a lot of time to explore the part of the country I'd called home for … well, my whole life. Thinking this would be an experience my mom would enjoy, I invited her to come with me.

When we checked in, the front-desk clerk handed me a key with a clunky wooden block that displayed the name of our room: Sugarlands. She kindly gestured toward the stairs and led us to a swanky room on the second floor. The large corner room welcomed us with a gorgeous wrought-iron bed, a huge Jacuzzi tub, and a wall of windows with sweeping views of the mountains that will forever have my heart.

Mom and I settled in and then went to Pigeon Forge for dinner. When we returned to Sugarlands that night, I filled the tub and we soaked our sore feet (because of course we'd been stomping all over Pigeon Forge to do some shopping!).

Despite being in one of the most beautiful places imaginable and sharing the experience with someone I loved, my mind struggled to focus on the blessings. Instead, my thoughts were fixated on how much I longed to share an experience like this with my future spouse. My desire for marriage was proving stronger than my sense of gratitude, and even as a stunning sunset covered the horizon and I splashed my toes in the hot, swirling water, all I could think was, *I can't wait to share this with* him.

My fixation on what I lacked had become a challenge during my single years, and this retreat was no exception. I look back fondly on those memories with Mom while also wanting to kindly tell *that* Rebecca that God had her story under his control and care.

You'll have to forgive me for a hard right turn here, but my time at Blue Mountain Mist was far from over.

After marrying Dustin, we were invited to speak at a marriage retreat. We were living in Mississippi at that time, so we were both excited to return to Tennessee and speak to a group from the church where we'd met each other years before.

After months of having the event on our calendar, I looked at Dustin across the kitchen island one day and asked, "Do you know where this marriage retreat thing is?"

He shook his head and said, "Brian said it's somewhere called *Blue ... Mist ... Blue Mountain* something. I'll have to ask him."

My eyes widened, and I almost jumped out of my skin.

"Blue Mountain Mist?"

He nodded, confused.

I told him the story about attending the retreat with Mom, staying in the Sugarlands room, and my hope to share an experience like that with my future husband ... with him.

Weeks later, when Dustin and I arrived at Blue Mountain Mist, the same front-desk clerk looked up at me and said, "Last name?"

"George," I replied, choking back tears. The significance of that moment wasn't lost on me; I was now checking in with a spouse and a married name.

After signing some paperwork, she grabbed the old familiar wooden block that held our key and, just like before, offered to walk us up to our room. My eyes strained to see what was written on the block, but her hand was covering the label. As she circled around her desk and started up the stairs, I whispered, "Surely not."

Lo and behold, she walked us straight to Sugarlands, the very same room that had been "randomly" (*wink, wink*) chosen for us unbeknownst to our friends who were hosting the retreat. As we walked inside, Dustin had a similar reaction to my first response when I walked into the room with my mom years earlier.

God is so generously intentional in the way he crafts each moment in our lives. Returning to Blue Mountain Mist was enough, but staying in Sugarlands made my heart so grateful for his provision.

When we surrender our stories to his care, he will craft them into something beyond what we could've dreamt up ourselves. For that reason, Blue Mountain Mist has become a bit of an Ebenezer stone, or stone of remembrance, reminding me how God answered my heart's cry.

Last year, Dustin and I planned to enjoy some quality time together for our anniversary. Going to Blue Mountain Mist was an easy choice for us, and although Sugarlands was booked, we were able to secure a room on the other side of the house.

One morning, while I was getting ready for the day, I could hear a family's discussion as they strolled outside my window. My attention turned to the little boy who trailed his parents. The child seemed so excited about this special adventure. Then he bent low to the ground and exclaimed, "Mom! Dad! Look at this bird I found!"

They smiled and proudly told him, "Good job, buddy! That's a beautiful bird!"

As they kept walking, tears filled my eyes. That's when I realized our *longing leads to more longing.*

You see, there was a day when all my heart longed for was to share the beauty of Sugarlands with my future spouse. *Then I did.* But now I ached to share the adventure with a child, the way those parents were doing outside my window. Getting the thing we want will never be enough. Almost immediately upon the realization of one goal, another desire *will* emerge. This is a by-product of our hurry-up world.

Dustin and I recently attended the same marriage retreat, and we were excited to spend time with old friends. Would you believe the attendant handed us keys to the same room we'd stayed in on our anniversary the year before? It was in mid-March, and, as I stumbled inside to unpack our luggage, I took a moment to glance through that familiar window. Below, a dogwood tree stood with its branches full of buds, each just days away from blooming. It filled my heart with hope to think that God is always at work in ways we can't see. We only have to surrender our desires to his greater plan and trust that he will make the path clear.

SPOILING A GOOD THING

To move forward, we must first understand what idolatry is and how to recognize when it creeps up in our lives.

An idol refers to anything that we elevate to an equal or higher importance than God in thought or action.

Let's read that again, slowly.

> Idolatry = when we elevate anything to an equal or higher importance than God … in thought or action.

The word that matters most in that sentence is *anything*. Simply put, idolatry is misplaced affection. We see it early in the Bible, when God gives Moses the law and instructs the Israelites, "You shall have no other gods before me" (Ex. 20:3).

ANYTHING MORE THAN GOD IS A LIE. ANYTHING LESS THAN GOD WILL LEAVE OUR HEARTS BEGGING FOR MORE. ANYTHING APART FROM GOD TAKES OUR EYES OFF MISSION.

In recent years, there has been an attack on foundational biblical truth, which has had a great effect on our hearts. Comfort and preferences have often prevailed. We have convinced ourselves that the *little sins* or *things we're microfixated on* don't offend our Creator.

> *Surely he doesn't care that I spend all my time and attention chasing that rung on the corporate ladder?*

You don't think he minds that I obsess and fantasize over the exact details of my future wedding, down to the shade of periwinkle that I'd like my bridesmaids to wear?

It's okay that all I find myself yearning for is a baby, right?

Desires such as these are good and *from God.* However, when our hearts become fixated more heavily on our earthly desires than on worshipping him, we have tread into dangerous waters. David tells us that when we *delight in the Lord*, he will *give us the desires of our heart* (see Ps. 37:4).

Also, Psalm 37:5 says we should *commit our way to him*, *trust in him*, and *he will act.*

As believers, we cling to this promise, trusting that he'll make things clear for us. But too many times we end up asking, "What's in it for me?"

We want so badly for God to give us wisdom, but we forget that we have a role to play in submitting to his will. We want the fruit without any of the pain, displeasure, and frustration that comes along with tilling, sowing, and waiting on the harvest.

I wonder if there's an area of idolatry that's rising in your heart as you read this chapter. Is there a focus in your life that you need to surrender to God?

The world tells us: **What I long for will satisfy me more fully than God.**

God tells us: **True satisfaction and contentment will only be found as I surrender my plans to God.**

The mind games we play have a lot to do with our circumstances. When we equate God's perceived goodness with our circumstances, we may find ourselves disappointed. But when we trust that he is MORE than enough for us *in ANY circumstance*, we can surrender and allow him to work in our hearts (2 Cor. 3:5).

Elisabeth Elliot wrote, "What God gives in answer to our prayers will always be the thing we most urgently need, and it will always be sufficient."[1]

In other words, true satisfaction will only be found in the safe arms of our Father. This is the only way.

Jesus modeled for us what it looks like to lay aside our own desires to pursue God's bigger plan. He made this clear in Luke 9 when he explained that, to be his disciples, we must deny ourselves, take up our crosses, and follow him daily.

> Anything more than God is a lie.
> Anything less than God will leave our hearts begging for more.
> Anything apart from God takes our eyes off mission.

Our desires, preferences, opinions, justifications, hopes, dreams, wishes, and concerns are often circumstantial and temporary in comparison to the overall plan of redemption that God is working together.

IF ONLY

Our minds wander in a hurry, don't they? We can so easily fixate on a future reality and put a plan in place to make it happen. Maybe it's a job promotion or a college degree. Maybe it's a specific wedding gown or a certain reception venue. Maybe it's a spouse or a child or a home or a car.

Whatever desire you're chasing, it can easily become an idol when you *worship* the *idea of* your hoped-for outcome.

You may be sitting with a relational or vocational longing and experiencing the lie of *if only*. Joy and contentment will never be found on the other side of your *if only*; rather, you will find them in surrendering the gap fully to God. When you find yourself filling in the chasm between where you are and where you want to be, use that as a prompt to pray for the meanwhile. God already knows how he intends to work all things together for your good and his glory (see Rom. 8:28).

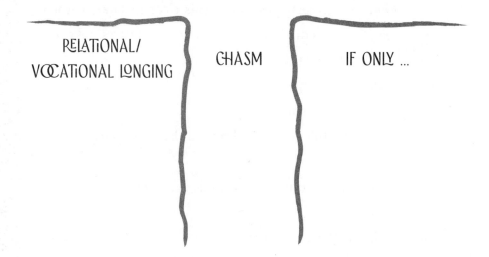

Now, I'm not saying it's wrong to dream. It's perfectly normal to feel anticipation or excitement about what God might do in a particular situation. I'm merely suggesting we consider that our limited perspective often leaves our hearts vulnerable to a sneaky form of idolatry.

It's likely you'll need to work through this exercise time and time again. We don't need stronger arms to pick things up and proudly hold them up before Jesus' gaze so we ensure he sees exactly how we hope he works next. We need a posture of humility to lay things down at his feet. Our fingers will ache at times from the tight grip we held, but there is such freedom and renewed joy on the other side of the release.

> WHATEVER DESIRE YOU'RE CHASING, IT CAN EASILY BECOME AN IDOL WHEN YOU _WORSHIP_ THE _IDEA_ _OF_ YOUR HOPED-FOR OUTCOME.

LONGING FOR EDEN

In the beginning, before the fall, God created us to live in perfect communion with him—free of sin, shame, guilt, and suffering.

After the fall, sin separated us from God. Sin is defined as anything, in *action* or *attitude*, that dishonors God. We live in a sin-stained world that longs for the return of Jesus. We ache for Eden because we were made for eternity. Deep down, our hearts know that we were meant to experience fellowship with God.

Jesus made a way for us to experience that fellowship when he came to dwell among us in his earthly ministry. He lived a perfect life, free of the sin we experience, and died a cruel death on the cross.

When Jesus cried, "It is finished," the veil separating the holy of holies in the temple was torn in two, top to bottom, symbolizing that Jesus' sacrifice was sufficient to make a way for our restored relationship with God (Matt. 27:50–51; John 19:30). Our sin—past, present, and future—was dealt with in finality. The separation we experienced from God before coming to a saving knowledge of Jesus was removed (see Eph. 2:1–10).

Jesus himself is the prize—not changed circumstances, what we long for, or seeing our wildest dreams come true. God has a great track record. Getting what we feel we're *too late* for doesn't actually fix the problem. There will always be something else to fix our eyes on, be tempted to worship, or put in the place of prominence meant for God alone. Lasting satiation is only found in one place. C. S. Lewis said it well: "If I find in myself a desire which no experience in this world can satisfy, the most probable explanation is that I was made for another world."[2]

Our hearts grasp at anything that resembles what we imagine our eventual perfect communion with God will be like. Dustin will often say that God is re-Edenizing the universe. In his perfect timing, every earthly desire will be met in him alone.

The problem is when God has placed us in a different story—*for now*. If you read my debut book *Do the Thing*, you'll remember my dear friend Danielle. Recently, we were discussing how we can easily feel too late for our lives.

"There is a chasm," Danielle said, "between *my* expected plan and having realistic expectations based on where God has planted my feet. God often places us in a different story than we would choose."

I looked at her and admitted, "I sometimes try to tell God what story I'd like him to choose for me."

The truth is that we don't get to stand over God's shoulder, as he holds the pen to our life story, and whisper demands in his ear about how we'd like our story to end. Revelation 3:15–18 tells us that he is either Lord of our lives or not Lord at all. There is no in-between, no negotiation of decision power, and no other way for the Christ follower to navigate life. We must trust that he will lead us toward his chosen path.

"SEARCH ME, GOD!" PRAYER

In this chapter, we've discovered key truths about idolatry and surrender. As we seek to put these truths into practice in our daily lives, let's return to our "Search Me, God!" prayer from Psalm 139:23–24 as a compass. Remember that God is omniscient (*he knows all things*). He knows the inner workings of your heart better than you do. This prayer is simply a way to repeat to God what you're recognizing as you examine your heart.

Search me, O God, and know my heart!
Try me and know my thoughts!
And see if there be any grievous way in me,
and lead me in the way everlasting!

Consider the following questions:

Recognize my thoughts: Where am I idolizing my longings in this current season?	
Reveal my sin: Is there a sin pattern (in word or deed) that has led to this idolatry?	

Realign my attitude: What do I need to surrender to God? How would surrender lead me back to a heart of worship that sees how God is at work on my behalf?	
Remember God's way: What is my next step as I lay down my idols in complete surrender?	

CASE STUDY

Now we're going to explore a case study to illustrate how idolatry and surrender could show up in your life. This time, we'll consider a vocational longing. Whether this example captures your current season or not, my prayer is that it helps you develop empathy for people who may be facing different circumstances.

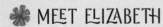 MEET ELIZABETH

Elizabeth is in her early thirties and has always had the strong desire to become an entrepreneur. Deep down, she believed that achievement in her career would provide her with validation and fulfillment, but this vocational longing became a form of idolatry that took precedence over her relationship with God.

CHALLENGES

Priorities: Elizabeth's relentless attitude in her entrepreneurship journey led her to prioritize her career over her faith. She equated her worth with achievement and often neglected time with God when she got swept up in her work.

Burnout and Discontentment: Despite remarkable success, Elizabeth continued to feel restless and discontent. The more she accomplished, the more she longed for greater success. This equation led to deep emotional burnout.

Strained Relationships: As she made progress in her business, Elizabeth eventually felt tension in her relationships with family and friends. She found it difficult to be intentional because of her commitments, and she missed meaningful connections as a result.

JOURNEY TO SURRENDER

One day, Elizabeth confided to a friend that she had placed her vocational goals above her relationship with God. Her pursuit of success had led to idolatry.

Elizabeth's friend encouraged her to spend time in prayer as she considered what it would look like to reevaluate her priorities. Together, they explored what Scripture says about putting God first (Matt. 6:33; 10:38–39; Col. 3:17).

Each morning, Elizabeth began spending time surrendering her career ambitions to God in prayer. She prayed for the strength to trust in God's timing and plan. She also set clear boundaries for how she would spend her time; she prioritized worship and being in community at her local church again. Elizabeth realized that to lay down this idol of achievement, she would need the encouragement and accountability of a healthy faith community.

CASE STUDY REFLECTION PROMPTS

1. In what way do you relate to Elizabeth's story?

2. What could you do this week to move from idolatry to surrender?

SCRIPTURE FOR REFLECTION

- Ephesians 2:1–10
- Romans 6:10–11; 8:28
- 2 Corinthians 3:5; 5:18
- Exodus 24:12–18; 34:14
- Psalm 37:4–5

QUESTIONS FOR REFLECTION

1. Do you relate to the story about my visits to Blue Mountain Mist? Have you ever satisfied one longing only to begin desiring something else?

2. Did God reveal an area in which you are struggling with idolatry?

3. Do you ever struggle with the lie of *if only*?

4. What step can you take to surrender your idols to
   God?

Chapter 3

DOUBT & HOPE

My hands were shaking as I pressed "End Call" and threw my cell phone across the coffee table—homemade of pallet wood—in the living room of my Knoxville, Tennessee, townhome. I stared at the ceiling, the room eerily quiet, and shook my head in disbelief. *I was going on a date with Dustin George.* *The* Dustin George that kids adored and who they wanted to hear stories from in Sunday school. *The* Dustin George who had a masterful gift for teaching God's Word. *The* Dustin George who'd prayed for me, encouraged me, and supported my ministry. *The* Dustin George who, to my surprise, had found his way into my heart after months of long phone conversations across the eight hours that separated us.

My ministry, at the time, often did volunteer work at St. Jude Children's Research Hospital in Memphis, Tennessee. For our next visit, we'd planned to dress up like Disney characters as we visited with patients and their families. Months earlier, while attending a pastor's conference in the area, Dustin had sent me a photo with St. Jude's campus in the distance and said it made him think of me. At that time, we'd made plans to "have dinner" the next time I was in town.

When I began planning another visit to St. Jude, Dustin asked if I'd like to spend time exploring Memphis together. What I didn't realize was that Brookhaven (the town in Mississippi where he lived at the time) was a four-hour drive from Memphis. *Four hours.* This man was willing to drive four hours and get a hotel room for the night just so he could spend the day with me. These were lengths that, I can assure you, no other man had gone to take me on a date.

A familiar feeling quickly settled into my heart. *Maybe this isn't really a date. He probably just sees me as a friend and wants to spend time catching up.*

My defenses were up, but when I called a girlfriend to tell her my plans, she said, "Rebecca, you do know this is a date, right? No man would drive four hours to have dinner and spend time with you if he had no intentions of pursuing you."

Even after discussing my plans with multiple friends, I still found my heart guarded against the possibility of disappointment. The equation was simple: low expectations equals no disappointment.

After volunteering at St. Jude, I met Dustin downtown. I vividly remember what it felt like to turn the corner, say hello, and give him a hug for the first time. Even still, my defenses were up, and I wondered if this whole scenario was too good to be true. We enjoyed Memphis BBQ for lunch, as one does when in the city of blues. Then we walked down Beale Street, enjoyed some gelato, and solved all the world's problems in a rich conversation that ranged from God to our upbringings to how we liked to dress a hamburger. It was a wonderful day, and as he dropped me off at my car and gave me a hug, we lingered a bit, not wanting to say goodbye.

My friend had been right. This *was*, in fact, a date.

If you're this far along in the book, you know how our story ended, and I couldn't be more honored to be the wife of THE Dustin George.

However, the doubts that welled in my heart at that time weren't any less real than yours. Even when we see God at work in and around us, we often discount forward progress to protect ourselves from more pain. Doubt is a lousy defense mechanism, but it often feels easier to cling to than hope, especially when we've experienced a string of disappointments in the past.

I, too, have wrestled to point myself in the direction of hope. However, when that is the case, I've learned that the object of my hope must shift. If it's placed on anything or anyone but God, it's fleeting. Maybe you know the feeling?

GOD IS NOT ON VACATION

Recently, Dustin and I vacationed in a stunning stretch of the Emerald Coast in Florida. Think powdery white sand and water as beautiful as the prettiest beach you can imagine. We've come to love this area, and as I sat in my beach chair, I tried to keep my nose in a novel, but it failed to capture my attention. My heart was in a plaintive state over some things happening in our current season, so I dog-eared my page, stared at the water, and waited for God to tell me what I should do next.

I'm embarrassed to admit how I've pictured God's perspective of my pain in the past. I sometimes imagined him as indifferent toward my doubts or struggles. I'd picture him relaxing at the Emerald Coast, feet propped up, completely unaware of my suffering and pain.

Now, I know this couldn't be further from the truth.

God is, in fact, not on vacation, ignoring our needs. He is orchestrating things we will never know behind the scenes of our lives. He grieves with us, is at work on our behalf, and is way, *way* ahead of the doubt we've yet to, but will, experience in the future.

As we explore the topic of doubt in this chapter, let's face the lies of the world head-on.

The world tells us: **I wonder if God will really come through for me.**

God tells us: **God is sovereign.**

Whether we're struggling with a relational or vocational longing, something is causing us to doubt it will all work out. We may sink in despair, believing he won't come through. *That* desire wasn't meant for us. Someone else will get it *before* we do. If we dig down to the bedrock of all these concerns, we're questioning the character of God, not our specific circumstances.

The sovereignty of God means that he is all-powerful and nothing is too difficult for him. He owns the cattle on a thousand hills, puts breath in our lungs, forces the planets to orbit the sun by his expressed word, and is the crafter of the cosmos. While there is no denying our doubts are real, they downplay the reality that God is *able*. If it be his will, he absolutely will shift, change, orchestrate, or reorder anything he wants for his glory.

No matter your circumstances, you are never too far gone or too far out of his reach. He is actively working on a master plan with your name on it, and he will reveal it in time. So, not only will God come through for you, but in his power he is already behind, beside, and before your very next breath.

PUT IT IN HIS HANDS (AGAIN)

Dustin and I were married in May 2019, around ten months before COVID-19 struck our nation. As Dustin led our church through the pandemic (and the chaos that ensued), I pursued a two-book traditional publishing contract and wrote my debut book, *Do the Thing*. I did this in the margins of a demanding full-time job, all while supporting Dustin's church ministry. It was anything but an easy first few years of marriage. The common thread that bonded us many days was our shared dream to move back home to Tennessee. Brookhaven was home, *for now*, we felt. But we longed to return to the loved ones and landscapes that were our own.

One day, I found a job posting in East Tennessee that caught my attention. I read the job description no less than twelve times and, finally, closed the browser. Tapping a pen on my desk, I thought about texting the link to Dustin. In fact, I had already drafted the message when God spoke clearly to me and said that I was not to bring up the opportunity to Dustin.

"But what if this is our opportunity to move home!" I exclaimed aloud in our otherwise quiet home.

I sensed the Holy Spirit say, *Don't you think if this is something you are to pursue that I am fully capable of bringing it to Dustin's attention as well?*

In obedience to God, I buried my head in my hands and deleted the text message I'd drafted to Dustin. It wasn't like I hadn't shared other job opportunities with him or moving to Tennessee wasn't something we considered often. Something just felt *different* this time.

Weeks passed. Two. *Long*. Weeks. We were on our way home from dinner when Dustin, hand on the steering wheel, peered at the stretch ahead and said, "Well, I saw a church in East Tennessee that is looking for a pastor."

The blood immediately drained from my face. "I know," I said, looking straight ahead. I explained to Dustin how I'd sensed that if it was an opportunity for us that he was to bring it up. We discussed the pros and cons, and we prayed for God to lead us. Then we agreed that if we continued to feel our hearts stirred the following week, Dustin would submit his résumé.

The next week, Dustin applied for the role, and then … *nothing.* Not a peep for six months. He stayed busy with his current position and responsibilities without being concerned about where this Tennessee opportunity might or might not lead.

I … well, I did not handle it so well.

Every month or so I'd scour the church's website to see if a new family had been added to their staff page. One day I thought to check the board where I had initially seen the job posted. The listing had been removed.

My heart dropped as tears fell. Clearly, *this wasn't for us.* Clearly, this was meant to prepare us, prepare me, to be able to entertain an opportunity to move home without letting it become an idol. I prayed, *God, I accept the lesson here and surrender my heart's desires back to you. Again.*

Months passed with no sign of the church calling a pastor. I told my best friend, Danielle, about the situation. To be as private as possible about the prayer concern, we began calling it Project V (short for Vonore, the town where the church is located). A handful of times when we were catching up, she would ask, "Any news from Project V?" I would shake my head no.

One day I was sitting on my parents' couch in East Tennessee, enjoying a morning cup of coffee with my mom, when Dustin texted me,

"Check your email." To my surprise, I opened my inbox to find a forwarded email from Jeff Amburn, the chairman of the search committee, telling us that after months of prayer, reviewing hundreds of résumés, and listening to various sermons, the committee had unanimously voted in favor of pursuing Dustin for the lead pastor position.

I was *shocked*.

As I was trying not to react, since I didn't want to let my parents into the excitement before there was anything to be excited about, Dustin texted me that he'd scheduled a call with Jeff.

That weekend we sat in our favorite barbeque restaurant in Pigeon Forge, and we both sensed that something was about to shift. Would we move back home? Was *this* the right opportunity? Did God have something completely different in store? We had no clue, but this visit to Tennessee just felt different. For *both* of us.

When we returned to Mississippi, we began what would be a five- or six-month process of conversations, phone calls, reference checks (on both sides), and, most importantly, prayer over this huge decision. There were moments along the way when I was booking flights for future speaking engagements and wasn't sure if I should purchase my outbound flight from Mississippi or Tennessee. I was just as sure that we would *stay* as I was that we would *go*. You know the feeling.

While on a walk near our church in Brookhaven one day, I told God in raw honesty that he knew the desires of my heart. He would work things together according to his plan for us. My biggest fear, our biggest fear, was somehow letting our desire to be back in Tennessee cloud our judgment. As I made my requests known to God (Phil. 4:6), the worship playlist I had piping through my AirPods switched to a newly released Maverick City Music song.

God will work it out
One thing I know
One thing I've found
God will work it out[1]

I listened to the song for another half hour on repeat as I continued walking and praying. This was the truth I would cling to until God made the answer clear: *God will work it out.*

Was his desire for us to stay in Mississippi?
God will work it out.

Would we move back home to Tennessee?
God will work it out.

How in the world would we afford the cost of living in East Tennessee with the insane amount of people relocating to the area?
God will work it out.

Would I launch my first book in Mississippi or Tennessee?
God will work it out.

What would it feel like to leave the only church I've known as pastor's wife and the friendships that made an especially difficult season more manageable?
God will work it out.

The in-between, almost-but-not-yet tension is where we live most of our days. This wondering (and wandering) comes along with faithfully following God's lead. I liken it to how the Israelites followed a pillar of cloud by day and a pillar of fire by night (Ex. 13:17–22). The pillars offered a visible guide to lead them on their exodus from Egypt. To have hope, their gaze had to be fixed upward. To gain direction and clarity, it was crucial they not lose sight of where God was taking them.

Our perspective isn't all that different from the Israelites, is it? These pillars of cloud and fire represented God's presence.

THE IN-BETWEEN, ALMOST-BUT-NOT-YET TENSION IS WHERE WE LIVE MOST OF OUR DAYS.

Now, because of Jesus' sacrifice for us, his presence dwells within his followers through the person of the Holy Spirit. We no longer have to fix our gaze on a pillar in the sky; God gives us wisdom and discernment through the Holy Spirit when we ask him (James 1).

While stuck in the in-between, Dustin and I would leave meetings with the search committee and ask one another, "Where are you?" We would each answer with a measure, zero to one hundred, of how confident we were that this move was the right decision for us. As you can imagine, the more we prayed, the more we oscillated between uncertainty and expectation.

Much like the Israelites wandering in the wilderness, our journey from doubt to hope is rarely, if ever, linear. Dustin and I didn't take our decision lightly. We continued asking God to confirm, through his Word, the right decision for us. We both refused to let our desire to be in Tennessee cloud our trust in God's plan for us.

One evening Dustin was sitting out by the firepit as the golden embers began to turn cold and gray. He was praying and begging God for direction. He stood up and went inside (I was long asleep for the night) but then came back out and looked up at the sky as if to say, *God! I'm here. Just please give me wisdom to know what to do.* As he gazed up, he saw the North Star shining brightly and thought, *There is a people up north who need help.* The path of the North Star, up and to the right of where our home was at the time, was also the path to the church.

Lord, I know they need help. That's clear. But am I the one to help them? he asked. God brought to mind a Scripture that Dustin recently had taught about in Acts 16. To set the scene, doors of ministry were continually closing for Paul. On his second missionary journey, he went through the region of Phrygia and Galatia (Acts 16:6), then Mysia where "they attempted to go into Bithynia, but the Spirit of Jesus did not allow them" (v. 7). When they passed by Mysia and went down to Troas, Paul received a vision in the night of a Macedonian man saying, "Come over to Macedonia and help us" (v. 9).

Even still, Dustin responded in prayer, *God, I know they* need *help. There's no question there! But am I, are we, the ones you're sending to do so?* Within a few days, Dustin was able to connect with a former staff member at the church and ask some important questions that he hoped would shed some light on the decision. They had a great conversation, but at the end, the man said, "Before I let you go, I have one more thing to share. Are you familiar with Paul's Macedonian call? Acts 16, I think it is?"

"Yes, yes, I am," Dustin said.

"Our former pastor shared with us that this town, well, it's kind of like Troas. All other roads get closed off, and then God sends you there to help. You don't simply *go* there. You're *sent* there."

As Dustin recounted the conversation to me, chills ran down my spine. God used an obscure detail from Paul's second missionary journey to give us a nudge toward going *home*. "Start packing, and get some moving quotes. Let's see what God has for us in Tennessee, babe!" Dustin said.

Maybe as you're reading these words, you're sitting outside in the cold, staring up at the sky, and begging God to speak to you. You may feel like you're hoping against hope as the weight of a big decision settles onto your shoulders.

In time, God will make his plans clear. It may be that he is calling you to faithfully stay where your feet are planted. Or maybe, just maybe, God is leading you in a new direction. Either way, he will walk with you on every step of your journey.

MUCH LIKE THE ISRAELITES
WANDERING IN THE WILDERNESS,
OUR JOURNEY FROM DOUBT TO
HOPE IS RARELY, IF EVER, LINEAR.

HOPE'S REQUIREMENT

Doubt inadvertently traps us between what *is* and what *could be*. There's no shortcut, no way out, and usually no way around the journey to hope. Sometimes we feel we're too old, we're too young, we don't have what it takes, or we've waited too long. I don't know what lie you're grasping as you hope for hope, but may it be a salve to your heart to know that God is at work on your behalf.

Jesus paid the full penalty for God's wrath by his finished work on the cross. As followers of Christ, our relationship with God the Father was restored because of Jesus. Our eternal hope rests in the empty grave that declares his sacrifice was sufficient to cover our sins (1 Pet. 1:3–5). Our inheritance is kept in heaven, and we live in the meanwhile before an eternity of worshipping him in awe of his holiness. We get to practice here on earth.

Hope's *prerequisite* is longing. It only exists when we're waiting for a desire to be fulfilled. We can white-knuckle our way through feeling too late, disappointed, let down, and not enough, wondering if it'll ever work out for us. But God gives us a better, more life-giving alternative.

We can anchor ourselves to his faithfulness. We can revel in his character and recall how we've seen it proven true in our lives.

As we reflect on the past or look to the future, two things commonly happen. When we consider the *past*, we *revise*. When we look to the *future*, we *catastrophize*. What do I mean?

When considering the past, we often remember things as more pleasant than they really were. This nostalgia leads us to imagine happier scenarios and ask, *What if I'd stayed? What might life look like now?* In these instances, we have to trace God's hand in the past to remind ourselves that he is just as much here in our *now*. His faithfulness is untethered from our desires. His faithfulness is *who he is*—his identity. Forever *and then some.*

Catastrophizing the future challenges the very same place in our hearts that glamorizes the past. *Will he show up for me like he did last time, or will I have to do this all on my own? Can I trust him? Will the fear ever go away?*

No matter what you're walking through—infertility, the loss of a loved one, going to *another* wedding for *another* friend, getting passed over for a promotion—he sees your struggle and is with you in it. To hope in a God we only know in part, we must cling to what we know is true of him.

Consider the following characteristics of God as you face your current circumstances. Allow this to be a guide you return to when you're struggling to cling to hope; fill in the blanks of each missing word in the verses.

Holy: God Is Perfect

- As obedient children, do not be conformed to the passions of your former ignorance, but as he who called you is _____, you also be holy in all your conduct, since it is written, "You shall be holy, for I am holy." (1 Pet. 1:14–16)
- For thus says the One who is high and lifted up, who inhabits eternity, whose name is _____: "I dwell in the high and holy place, and also with him who is of a contrite and lowly spirit, to revive the spirit of the lowly, and to revive the heart of the contrite." (Isa. 57:15)

Infinite: God Is Limitless

- Great is our Lord, and _____ in power; his understanding is beyond measure. (Ps. 147:5)
- Have you not known? Have you not heard? The LORD is the everlasting God, the Creator of the ends of the earth. He does not _____ or grow weary; his understanding is unsearchable. (Isa. 40:28)

Immutable: God Never Changes

- Jesus Christ is the same yesterday and today and _____. (Heb. 13:8)
- Every good gift and every perfect gift is from above, coming down from the Father of lights, with whom there is no _____ or shadow due to change. (James 1:17)

Self-Sufficient: God Doesn't Have Any Needs

- For as the Father has _____ in himself, so he has granted the Son also to have life in himself. (John 5:26)
- The God who _____ the world and everything in it, being Lord of heaven and earth, does not live in temples made by man. (Acts 17:24)

Omniscient: God Is All-Knowing

- Whenever our heart condemns us, God is greater than our heart, and he knows _____. (1 John 3:20)

- Even before a word is on my tongue, behold, O LORD, you know it _____. (Ps. 139:4)

Omnipotent: God Is All-Powerful

- What is the immeasurable greatness of his _____ toward us who believe, according to the working of his great might. (Eph. 1:19)
- Behold, I am the LORD, the God of all flesh. Is _____ too hard for me? (Jer. 32:27)

Omnipresent: God Is Everywhere

- The eyes of the LORD are in every _____, keeping watch on the evil and the good. (Prov. 15:3)
- You hem me in, behind and before, and lay your _____ upon me. Such knowledge is too wonderful for me; it is high; I cannot attain it. (Ps. 139:5–6)

Wise: God Is Full of Wisdom

- The LORD by _____ founded the earth; by understanding he established the heavens. (Prov. 3:19)
- If any of you lacks wisdom, let him ask God, who gives _____ to all without reproach, and it will be given him. (James 1:5)

Faithful: God Is Trustworthy

- Know therefore that the LORD your God is God, the _____ God who keeps covenant and steadfast love with those who love him and keep his commandments, to a thousand generations. (Deut. 7:9)

- If we confess our sins, he is _____ and just to forgive us our sins and to cleanse us from all unrighteousness. (1 John 1:9)

Good: God Is Kind

- Oh give thanks to the LORD, for he is _____, for his steadfast love endures forever! (Ps. 107:1)
- And we know that for those who love God all things work together for _____, for those who are called according to his purpose. (Rom. 8:28)

Just: God Is Right

- The Rock, his work is perfect, for all his ways are _____. A God of faithfulness and without iniquity, just and upright is he. (Deut. 32:4)
- Righteousness and _____ are the foundation of your throne; steadfast love and faithfulness go before you. (Ps. 89:14)

Merciful: God Is Compassionate toward Us

- Be merciful, even as your Father is _____. (Luke 6:36)
- Blessed be the God and Father of our Lord Jesus Christ! According to his great _____, he has caused

us to be born again to a living hope through the resurrection of Jesus Christ from the dead. (1 Pet. 1:3)

Gracious: God Spares the Guilty

- For by _____ you have been saved through faith. And this is not your own doing; it is the gift of God, not a result of works, so that no one may boast. (Eph. 2:8–9)
- But he said to me, "My _____ is sufficient for you, for my power is made perfect in weakness." Therefore I will boast all the more gladly of my weaknesses, so that the power of Christ may rest upon me. For the sake of Christ, then, I am content with weaknesses, insults, hardships, persecutions, and calamities. For when I am weak, then I am strong. (2 Cor. 12:9–10)

Glorious: God Is Great

- And the Word became flesh and dwelt among us, and we have seen his _____, glory as of the only Son from the Father, full of grace and truth. (John 1:14)
- O LORD, our Lord, how _____ is your name in all the earth! You have set your glory above the heavens. (Ps. 8:1)

As a Christ follower, you have access to *this* God every day through the person of the Holy Spirit (Rom. 8). This side of heaven, we see through a mirror dimly (1 Cor. 13:12), and we know God only in part. But as we hope, not only for today but for the future, we know that one day he will return and set all things right.

One day when we no longer struggle with doubt, and eternity with him is our agenda, there will be no need for hope. We will be free of pain, weakness, rejection, hurt, and despair. We will *never* feel *too late* again because we will spend forever in awe of his holiness. Nothing else will matter anymore.

In the meantime, we get to practice hope as we remember that he longs to be gracious to us (Isa. 30:18). God sees through the eyes of eternity already, and we can rest in the *unknown* that has been *known* by him for generations on generations.

Maybe you feel as if you'll never get your turn. You're not alone. The Bible is filled with stories of those who faced challenging circumstances that could cause anyone to lose hope.

- Moses faced struggles that would cause any good leader to throw in the towel.
- Ruth was a widow who chose to follow God's lead and stay with Naomi.
- David waited fifteen years after he was anointed before becoming king.
- Job persevered despite agonizing loss.
- The woman in Luke 8 had been bleeding for twelve years (can you imagine?) before Jesus healed her.
- Sarah was ninety years old when her son Isaac was born.
- It's suggested that Mary was fifteen or sixteen when she learned she'd give birth to the Savior of the world.

Absolutely nothing is too difficult for God (see this proven true in Mary's story by reading Luke 1). Elisabeth Elliot said it well when she stated, "In the words of a Portuguese proverb, 'God writes straight with crooked lines,' and He is far more interested in our getting where He wants us to be than we are in getting there. He does not discuss things with us. He *leads* us faithfully and plainly as we trust Him and simply do the next thing."[2]

We tend to think our plan is best (Prov. 21:2), but letting go of our expectations and preferences allows us to be open to his purposes for us. When you're struggling to turn from your doubt and grasp for hope, ask God to help your unbelief (Mark 9:24).

"SEARCH ME, GOD!" PRAYER

As we apply the truths we've discovered about doubt and hope, let's return to our "Search Me, God!" prayer as a compass to direct us. Remember that God is omniscient (*he knows all things*), so he knows the inner workings of your heart better than you do. This prayer from Psalm 139:23–24 is simply a way to repeat back to God what you're recognizing as you examine your heart.

Search me, O God, and know my heart!
Try me and know my thoughts!
And see if there be any grievous way in me,
and lead me in the way everlasting!

Consider the following questions:

Recognize my thoughts: Where am I struggling to believe God is going to show up?	
Reveal my sin: Is there a sin pattern (in word or deed) that has led to this doubt?	
Realign my attitude: Where in my life do I need to remember that God is working on my behalf?	
Remember God's way: What is my next step as I place my hope in God?	

CASE STUDY

Now we're going to explore a case study that I hope can help you see how doubt and hope could show up in your life. This time, we'll consider an example of relational longing. Whether this example captures your current season or not, my prayer is that it helps you develop empathy for people who may be facing different circumstances.

 MEET ANITA

Anita is in her midsixties and has longed to experience the joy of becoming a grandmother. Her daughter and son-in-law have faced years of infertility and a recent miscarriage, leaving Anita with doubt and confusion about how she can best support her child and hope for the future.

CHALLENGES

Weight of Loss: Anita's desire for grandchildren has always been a source of joy in her life. The recent miscarriage left her feeling the weight of continued disappointment and loss. Her daughter's loss also became her own.

Helplessness: As she watched her daughter and son-in-law's emotional roller coaster, she grappled with feelings of helplessness. The most painful part for her was that she couldn't make their pain go away. She couldn't *fix it*, so she found herself questioning God's plan and asking how she should best support and encourage the grieving couple.

Fatigue: This relational longing tested her faith, and she found herself exhausted from a lack of sleep and from praying until she wasn't sure what else to pray. Her friendship with Jesus suffered because she began to reinterpret God's faithfulness in light of her daughter's loss rather than lean on his faithfulness *in* the loss.

JOURNEY TO HOPE

Anita recognized that her doubt was not just affecting her personally but was also impacting her relationship with Jesus. She decided to go before God and acknowledge her feelings, remembering that he was with her in the pain. She also turned to her local church and sought counseling on how to best move forward. There she was encouraged to remember that God's plans are beyond human understanding at times.

She initiated a conversation with her daughter and son-in-law to make sure they understood she was there to support them emotionally and pray specifically for them. She knew that one of the best ways she could love them was simply by listening to their hearts. As she began to understand the struggles they were facing, her prayers shifted from merely asking God for a specific outcome to pleading for his guidance and peace for their next steps.

As things progressed, Anita discovered that hoping in God didn't mean abandoning the desire of her heart. Rather, she began surrendering to his greater plan and trusting in his sovereignty over all things. Uncertainty and hope could coexist, she discovered, as she trusted God to write her story.

CASE STUDY REFLECTION PROMPTS

1. In what way do you relate to Anita's story?

2. What could you do this week to move from doubt to hope?

SCRIPTURE FOR REFLECTION

- Exodus 13:17–22
- James 1
- Acts 16
- 1 Peter 1:3–5
- Proverbs 21:2

QUESTIONS FOR REFLECTION

1. Where in your life are you weary of disappointment? Is that disappointment contributing to your doubt?

2. Have you ever been afraid to hope because you don't want to be disappointed?

3. What attribute of God is the most encouraging to you in your doubt?

4. Do you struggle to remember that God's sovereignty doesn't hinge on your circumstances?

Chapter 4

FEAR & CONFIDENCE

One Mother's Day weekend, Sunday evening activities were canceled at the church, giving Dustin and me a free night (a rarity in our home, as you can imagine). I sat on the couch and mindlessly scrolled on my phone.

"Want Thai food?" I mumbled to Dustin across the room.

"Sure," he said.

I gave our favorite local place a call and got in the car, looking forward to the chicken pad thai that awaited me.

When I walked inside, I was greeted with a warm smile by the man at the counter. "Rebecca?" he cheerfully asked.

"That's me."

He rang up our order, and as I gently pushed my credit card into the machine, he smiled as it beeped and said, "Are you a mother?"

Gut punch. I know. He meant absolutely *nothing* by it, which I can confirm by how kind he's been to me on countless occasions I've picked up food, but for some reason his inquiry stirred up something in the pit of my stomach. I wasn't upset with him, per se, but I found my mind spinning with more thoughts than his question seemed to necessitate.

I paused as a lump formed in my throat.

"No," I said in a friendly tone.

"Well, I have no doubt you are a mother in many ways and to many people, so we celebrate you, too, today." He smiled and handed me my receipt.

I nodded in agreement, thanked him, grabbed the steamy goodness, and walked back to the car. I slumped into the driver's seat of my vehicle as I continued to process his question (and his attempted encouragement). What made me anxious was wondering if my honest answer to his question was enough. He merely wanted to honor and celebrate moms on Mother's Day, a good desire, and yet something in me felt offended. Not by him, but by the season I'd been handed in comparison to my peers. I absolutely desire to have children one day, but that day is not *to*day. So there I was, noodles in hand, feeling *too late* in a hurry-up world.

Maybe you can relate. It's common that we'll bump into conversations that tap into our longing in a way we were not expecting. At the root, what happens in our nervous system—the dump of cortisol (the stress hormone) we feel in our bodies—can often be traced back to fear.

When fear is expressed in unhealthy ways, it often looks like anxiety, anger, or annoyance.

> Anxiety makes us feel like we're supposed to have a *different answer to the question the world asks us, especially if we want another person's approval.*

> Anger, although understandable at times, *rises when we assume other people are the experts in our story.* (Spoiler alert: They're not.)

Annoyance occurs when we place unfair expectations on anyone who might say, do, or express something in a way that goes against our preferences.

Sometimes we can even make others feel stupid for asking the question. All of these unhealthy expressions stem from the fear that God is unaware of or indifferent toward our desires.

Make no mistake: He sees us and knows our fears and our hopes. He also has the answers to them. His plans may look nothing like what we desire. But his plans are good and right, despite our fears.

As we consider fear in this chapter, we must remember God's truth.

The world tells us: **The outcome of what *might be* is terrifying.**

God tells us: **My confidence is rooted in my *fixed identity* as a Christ follower.**

I vividly remember the feeling in my gut when I woke up on my twenty-fifth birthday. I'd been going to countless wedding showers, bachelorette parties, and baby showers, trying my darndest (yes, I looked, it's a word!) to show up for friends while they were receiving everything I wanted. I sat up in bed, crying. Twenty-four, twenty-three, twenty-two—those years hadn't seemed so bad. But twenty-five felt like a gut punch. This was a benchmark, the age at which I'd always imagined I'd be a wife and a mother.

Most women in my mother's generation already had kids, or were well on their way, by the age of twenty-five. Often, I would mentally calculate how much longer I had before I would be the age my mom was when she gave birth to me (twenty-eight), as if that were the only timeline available for me. Super unhealthy thought pattern, I'm aware. And let's be clear: ZERO of that pressure came from my mother. I put it all on myself!

That morning, I kept doing the math: *If I got married right now, I could be married for three years before I turn twenty-eight.* There was only one problem: I wasn't dating anyone, and I had no potential suitors in sight.

I spent the majority of my birthday sulking rather than savoring how God was at work in my life. I was leading a thriving ministry, had a fantastic job, lived in a gorgeous townhome near the bank of the Tennessee River, and walked in community with some amazing women at my local church. It was a beautiful season of life for which I thank God. He was providing in ways I didn't know I needed, and I didn't even recognize those provisions at the time.

The more I thought and prayed that day, the more I realized that my singleness wasn't what was weighing on me. It was the wondering *how much longer* I'd be single in the future.

Now, I realize you may be reading this book in a completely different life phase. You may be sixty-five, not twenty-five. While I don't know your story, I share my experience with the hope that you might recognize a similar pattern of thinking.

Where do you find yourself fearful, asking God *how much longer* you will have to endure the waiting?

MAKE NO MISTAKE: HE SEES US AND KNOWS OUR FEARS AND OUR HOPES. HE ALSO HAS THE ANSWERS TO THEM.

When we see our fears in light of the gospel, it's easy to see that God is not leaving us hanging. We don't have to wonder when he will show up for us. Quite the contrary! He has already done so: Jesus came to bear the full penalty of our sin on the cross, and he rose again victorious, showing that his sacrifice was sufficient to restore our relationship with him if we repent of our sin and surrender to his lordship. Jesus did this to make the abundant life possible that he talked about in John 10:10. We don't have to fear the future because we know who is seated on the throne (Heb. 10:12–13) and who is coming back to restore all things (John 14:1–3). These truths should cause our hearts to rejoice in his goodness and grace over our lives. As Christians, we have a fixed identity in Christ that will not shift from season to season. It's not fickle, and it doesn't change when we feel too late or experience disappointment.

This next illustration requires a quick trip back to economics class. Do you remember studying fixed versus variable costs? Let's have a quick refresher.

> A **fixed cost** is sure, finished, and doesn't typically change over the course of time. Your rent amount on an apartment in a yearlong lease or a fixed-rate mortgage payment are good examples of fixed costs.

> A **variable cost** is something that changes over time with economic shifts. The price of gas, groceries, or toiletries are good examples of variable costs.

We can view our identity as either fixed or variable. If we look to the world (or to other people) for validation of our identity, we will struggle to kick our feet fast enough and flail our arms with enough strength to bob our heads above the surface. Simply put, we *will* drown in the turbulent waters. Minute to minute, the world can make us feel valued or devalued, worthy or unworthy, loved or unloved.

But as followers of Christ, we can rest in the fixed identity we have in him. We are always valued, worthy, and loved in his eyes. That truth never wavers. Why? Because of Jesus' sacrifice, his righteousness has been applied to our lives (2 Cor. 5:21). The crazy part? It's been applied past, present, *and* future.

When God looks at our past wounds, he sees a *righteous daughter.* When he sees our present fear, temptation, and sin, he sees a *righteous daughter.* When he looks forward to every future slip, secret sin, or upcoming failure, he sees a *righteous daughter.*

Does that mean we abuse grace in response to our fear?

Absolutely not.

But as we begin to wonder *why* our life isn't going the way we imagined, or when we begin to feel captive to another person's thoughts about our current season, we can remember that our allegiance is to an audience of One. We can obey in faith and move forward in confidence, taking every step with worship and gratitude for what he's already done in our lives and for what he's doing right now for us (even if we can't yet see what that is).

When a random comment, a well-intentioned word of encouragement, or an opinionated family member's thoughts leave us with a twinge of fear, we have a choice: fear God or fear man (Gal. 1:10).

Put another way: Are you focusing on your fixed identity in Christ or the variable identity people in your life assign to you? Only one will last. Only one will never change.

When in fear or doubt, cling to what God says is true about you. It's the surest foundation we'll ever have.

IDENTITY CRISIS

Over the last five years or so, I've gone through a great deal of change. Arguably, at the time this book is being written, collectively as a people, we all have. However, from 2019 to 2024 I got married, left a job, began a new job, left a church, joined my husband in ministry, became a pastor's wife, secured a book deal, experienced a global pandemic, moved back to Tennessee, started a new job, left another church, *and, and, and* ... it's been a lot. A whole lot. I bet you could say the same about your life. Life is marked by change.

At one point, I took a change inventory test. It was designed to assess the amount of stress and change the user has experienced in every domain of life. A score of 0–100 was deemed a manageable amount of change. A score of 101–200 was considered a *significant* amount of change. A score above 200 signified that it would be wise to seek counseling and work through the stress these changes had caused.

My score was 260!

Maybe you relate to enduring a stressful season. When multiple areas of life are shifting and changing, we feel no sense of control. We can even experience a bit of an identity crisis. I imagined my life as a bunch of scattered puzzle pieces throughout this season of change. It took a while to put everything back together.

As I spent time in God's Word and asked him to show me more of who he is, I found comfort in the truth that, even while I was in a season of turmoil, God never changes. That means everything we know to be true about *us* never changes either. I'm not referring to our individual personalities, tendencies, or anything that can be shaped by the world. I'm talking about our unchanging position as beloved children of a holy God.

> WHEN IN FEAR OR DOUBT, CLING TO WHAT GOD SAYS IS TRUE ABOUT YOU. IT'S THE SUREST FOUNDATION WE'LL EVER HAVE.

Because of the gospel, our identity is sure and unchanging. It's fixed in every season of our lives, including when we feel too late or fear that we will have to keep waiting. Consider the following character traits of the Christ follower. Fill in the blanks in the Scriptures below, and return to this set of reminders in moments when you're struggling with confidence.

Child of God: You Are God's Kid

- But to all who did receive him, who believed in his name, he gave the right to become _____ of God. (John 1:12)
- The Spirit himself bears witness with our spirit that we are _____ of God. (Rom. 8:16)

Chosen: Before the Dawn of Time, God Chose YOU

- But you are a _____ race, a royal priesthood, a holy nation, a people for his own possession, that you may proclaim the excellencies of him who called you out of darkness into his marvelous light. (1 Pet. 2:9)

- Even as he _____ us in him before the foundation of the world, that we should be holy and blameless before him. (Eph. 1:4)

Ambassador: You Represent
God to Others

- Therefore, we are _____ for Christ, God making his appeal through us. We implore you on behalf of Christ, be reconciled to God. (2 Cor. 5:20)
- But our _____ is in heaven, and from it we await a Savior, the Lord Jesus Christ. (Phil. 3:20)

Heir: You Are a Coheir with Jesus

- And if children, then _____—heirs of God and fellow heirs with Christ, provided we suffer with him in order that we may also be glorified with him. (Rom. 8:17)
- So that being justified by his grace we might become _____ according to the hope of eternal life. (Titus 3:7)

New Creation: Because of
Salvation, You Are Transformed

- Therefore, if anyone is in Christ, he is a new _____. The old has passed away; behold, the new has come. (2 Cor. 5:17)

- For we are his workmanship, _____ in Christ Jesus for good works, which God prepared beforehand, that we should walk in them. (Eph. 2:10)

Redeemed: You Are Saved
by the Blood of Jesus

- In him we have _____ through his blood, the forgiveness of our trespasses, according to the riches of his grace. (Eph. 1:7)

- You were _____ from the futile ways inherited from your forefathers, not with perishable things such as silver or gold, but with the precious blood of Christ, like that of a lamb without blemish or spot. (1 Pet. 1:18–19)

Friend: You Are a Friend of God

- No longer do I call you servants, for the servant does not know what his master is doing; but I have called you _____, for all that I have heard from my Father I have made known to you. (John 15:15)

- And the Scripture was fulfilled that says, "Abraham believed God, and it was counted to him as righteousness"—and he was called a _____ of God. (James 2:23)

Conqueror: You Live in
the Victory of Christ

- No, in all these things we are more than _____ through him who loved us. (Rom. 8:37)

- For everyone who has been born of God overcomes the world. And this is the _____ that has overcome the world—our faith. (1 John 5:4)

Temple: The Holy Spirit
Lives within You

- Or do you not know that your body is a _____ of the Holy Spirit within you, whom you have from God? You are not your own. (1 Cor. 6:19)
- What agreement has the _____ of God with idols? For we are the temple of the living God; as God said, "I will make my dwelling among them and walk among them, and I will be their God, and they shall be my people." (2 Cor. 6:16)

Servant: You Serve God Alone

- For am I now seeking the approval of man, or of God? Or am I trying to please man? If I were still trying to please man, I would not be a _____ of Christ. (Gal. 1:10)
- Knowing that from the Lord you will receive the inheritance as your reward. You are _____ the Lord Christ. (Col. 3:24)

Disciple: You Are His Follower

- Go therefore and make _____ of all nations, baptizing them in the name of the Father and of the Son and of the Holy Spirit. (Matt. 28:19)

- So Jesus said to the Jews who had believed him, "If you abide in my word, you are truly my _____." (John 8:31)

Because God, in his immutability, says these things about you, guess what? They will never change. In the face of profound transition, uncertainty, trauma, grief, disappointment, or fear, these statements about your identity will remain true. They are not based on circumstances but on your *fixed* position in Christ.

VISCERAL RESPONSES

It's not uncommon for people to ask if I have children. Recently, I was speaking at a conference and, as often happens, an attendee gazed down at my wedding ring and asked if I had any kids. That day, I didn't have the energy to explain our season to her and didn't feel the need to justify *why* we didn't have children yet. I merely answered with one word: *no*. It was all the conversation required. She was a stranger after all. But as we kept talking at the merch table, something in my heart felt like I owed her more of an explanation.

The more we talked, the more I felt it well up in me. A mix of emotions that my body had been conditioned to feel when I was asked questions like this.

I bet you can relate.

This visceral response that happens in our body is a flight-or-fight response. Epinephrine, the adrenaline hormone, is released in our bodies when we feel anxious. I wish I could give you a step-by-step program to help your body avoid these survival responses, but there is a way we can honor the person asking the question *and* honor our season of longing.

We can pre-decide how we will answer uncomfortable questions.

Does that negate or cancel the biochemical response that happens in our bodies? Absolutely not, but it does short-circuit the response and hopefully lessen its impact.

What do I mean?

Whether it's having children, advancing in your career, getting married, becoming a grandparent, or any heart's desire that feels a little tender for you, let's spend some time processing these questions so we can anticipate our emotional response and prepare a script that will help us answer without going into survival mode.

First, take some time below to explore what questions elicit a flight-or-fight response in you.

SAMPLE QUESTIONS:

- Do you have children yet?
- Are you dating anyone?
- How is that job going?

What would you add to this mix? What questions stir up big feelings or emotions in you?

Reflect on how the question makes you feel. Does it often bring up fear or another emotion (embarrassment, disappointment, rejection, sadness) in you?

Next, let's explore some suggested scripts for how to respond in these conversations. It's likely that not all of them will resonate with your personality, but consider which one(s) might feel the most honoring to God and your situation.

SUGGESTED SCRIPTS

Having language to describe our season helps us in these moments of uncertainty and enables us to respond to others in healthy ways. It gives us greater confidence while honoring the curiosity in someone's question. Check the box(es) below of the responses that feel honoring to your situation.

□ **When are you having children?**

We are trusting in God's perfect timing for our family. Right now, we are focusing on our marriage while also praying for the future. We invite you to join us in prayer!

□ **Are you dating anyone?**

I appreciate you asking, but right now, I am not dating anyone. I am confident God has a plan for my life, and I'm patiently and excitedly waiting for him to reveal the right person in his timing.

☐ **Have you found a new job yet?**

My search continues, but in the meantime I'm grateful for the opportunities God has given me. I'm remaining open to God's guidance. Will you join me in prayer about that?

☐ **Don't you want to settle down?**

I don't believe I'll be single forever. Right now, I'm savoring this season and can see God at work in all areas of my life.

☐ **Why can't you find a man to marry? Are you even trying?**

Marriage is a gift from God, and I can't wait to experience that joy when the time is right. For now, I'm focused on my growing relationship with Jesus so that I'm prepared when God sends the right man into my life. Will you pray with me about that?

☐ **Have you considered fertility treatments or adoption?**

We're open to all possibilities, and we're seeking God's guidance in our journey. We invite you to join us in prayer.

☐ **What do you think is the next step in your career?**

My career is important to me, and I am also mindful of maintaining a balanced life. I'm trusting in God's guidance, which is helping me find contentment in both my job and my personal life.

☐ **Don't you feel left out?**

It can be challenging at times to watch others experience the stage of life I desire, but I'm finding contentment in my current season by seeking God's purposes for me and cherishing the unique blessings of this time.

☐ **Aren't you afraid of being alone?**

Being alone is a very real fear; however, no matter what season I'm in, I'm never alone because of my relationship with Jesus. This season can be filled with personal growth and service if I keep my eyes fixed on Jesus.

Remember, the person asking the question probably has good intentions and genuinely wants you to experience joy and fulfillment. However, that doesn't dismiss the unintentional hurt that can accompany their words.

FEAR CAN LOOK LIKE GRIEF

There is no love *quite* like grandparent love. I was a couple of months away from getting married to Dustin in the spring of 2019, and I found myself at my grandparents' home in East Tennessee. If you read my book *Do the Thing*, this is the grandfather who took the oil painting class with me. That experience taught me so much about what it looks like to move forward even when we're scared and unsure of the outcome.

I sat in their kitchen, steamy mug of coffee between my hands, and between bites of honeybun cake we caught up on work, projects they had going on around the farm, and (maybe most importantly) the romantic lives of all four of their granddaughters—myself included. Shockingly, after all that time of being single and hoping for marriage, at long last, I would be the first Ladd granddaughter to marry. Believe me, I was the *most* surprised of us all!

At that time, only one of the three other granddaughters was seeing someone. As we were all approaching our late twenties, I knew Mamaw and Papaw longed to see us all find someone to share our lives with. I remember my grandmother saying, "I just want so badly for the three of them to find godly men to marry. Where are they? I know it's not for lack of trying."

Papaw followed with a tongue-in-cheek joke about how maybe they should join farmersonly.com to meet their match.

After bantering back and forth, I said, "God is preparing a man for each of them. We have to be patient and pray for him. I promise you that absolutely no one … *no one* grieves their singleness more than they do. They live in the reality of it *every day*. What is most helpful to them is showing genuine interest in where God is at work in and around them. Ask how you can pray and support *those* things."

Sometimes when we fear that God might not provide, we grieve the perceived outcomes of our lives. Unlike God, we are not omniscient. We don't know how the story will end. BUT GOD DOES.

We often grieve things like the possibility of growing old without a spouse, not experiencing the joys of becoming a parent, or missing out on a host of other situations we long for. Those are valid thoughts and should be processed. However, when we let our minds ruminate on the possible outcomes for too long, we can waste a lot of time and energy fearing a future that may or may not be the reality God has chosen for us.

Instead of staying stuck in grief, let's work through a process that will enable us to move forward where God *is* blessing us.

First, we have to name the reality of the future grief we might experience. In a sense, we're *pre-grieving* before it's our reality. There is, of course, a probability that the thing we're imagining as the worst-case scenario might come true. However, we know God will sustain us wherever he leads. At this stage, it's important to name that worst-case scenario. A few examples might include:

I'll never marry.

I'll never become a parent (or grandparent).

I'll never achieve career success.

I'll never be able to retire.

Take some time to write down your worst-case scenarios. This is the first step toward acknowledging the outcomes we fear the most.

Second, we need to acknowledge the emotion that wells up in us when we consider the situation we're pre-grieving. Maybe when you imagine the worst-case scenario, you feel fear, sadness, or anxiety. Recognize each emotion that surfaces, and allow yourself to feel. Those emotions are real and God-given! Believe me, as a girl who rarely cries in front of others and who used to avoid conflict like the plague, this emotional processing can feel uncomfortable. You may want to invite a trusted friend, counselor, or mentor into this process with you.

Take some time to name and feel the emotions that surface when you consider your fears.

Third, and most importantly, we must release these emotions and grief to the God who is in control. He did not give us a spirit of fear, but of power, love, and a sound mind (2 Tim. 1:7). The Enemy would love nothing more than to distract us from seeing how God is at work in our lives. So, we want to release every obstacle that could prevent us from moving forward with clarity (2 Cor. 10:5).

Pray alongside me as we give our worst-case scenarios to God:

God, I trust that you know the end from the beginning (Isa. 46:10). These worst-case scenarios have been a distraction, and I want to surrender them to your careful control. Fill in the gaps of my doubt with trust that you will provide in a way that brings you honor and glory (Rom. 8:28). Give me your peace and wisdom as I trust in you.

Recently, I got to attend the wedding of one of the Ladd grand-daughters. As I'm typing these words, now all *four* of us are married to men who love God and love us. Attending Lauren's wedding was a powerful display of God's provision. I sat in front on the bride's side with my family, which just so happened to be where the vocalist and string band were placed. As a new song began, out poured the old hymn "Holy Ground."

We are standing on holy ground
And I know that there are angels all around
Let us praise Jesus now
We are standing in His presence on holy ground[1]

The song beautifully expressed that God was with us, and with them, as they entered into a marriage covenant. It truly felt as if we were standing on holy ground. The impact of answered prayer was not lost on me. God had brought James to Lauren. His presence was there, and her longing to be married had been satisfied. Fear of being alone vanished as two became one.

I couldn't help but reflect on the day when I had grieved with Mamaw and Papaw over the singleness of their granddaughters. We could now rejoice over how God had always been at work in Lauren's life.

WE DON'T KNOW HOW THE STORY WILL END. *BUT GOD DOES.*

"SEARCH ME, GOD!" PRAYER

As we apply the truths we've discovered about fear and confidence, let's return to our "Search Me, God!" prayer as a compass to direct us. Remember that God is sovereign (*he is Lord over creation*), and we can take confidence in knowing he is at work. This prayer is simply a way to repeat back to God what you're recognizing as you examine your heart.

Search me, O God, and know my heart!
Try me and know my thoughts!
And see if there be any grievous way in me,
and lead me in the way everlasting!

Consider the following questions:

Recognize my thoughts: Where am I experiencing fear in my longing?	
Reveal my sin: Is there a sin pattern (in word or deed) that has led to this fear?	
Realign my attitude: Where in my life do I need to remember that my confidence is rooted in my *fixed identity* as a Christ follower?	
Remember God's way: What is my next step as I release my fears to God?	

CASE STUDY

Now we're going to explore a case study that I hope can help you see how fear and confidence could show up in your life. This time, we'll consider an example of relational longing. Whether this example captures your current season or not, my prayer is that it helps you develop empathy for people who may be facing different circumstances.

 MEET MADI

Madi is a young woman in her midtwenties who recently began her career journey as a marketing professional. Alongside her budding career, she has a deep desire for marriage and family. Balancing her career and remaining open to meeting new people has been a challenge. At a friend's recent wedding, she began to fear getting left behind by her friends who are marrying and starting families.

CHALLENGES

Anxiety: Madi yearns for a life partner and questions why God hasn't provided someone for her. The fear of never marrying leaves her with deep insecurity and anxious thoughts.

Fear of the Future: While establishing her budding career in marketing, Madi often faces self-doubt. Her desire to excel in her career seems to clash with her longing for marriage, leading her to fear what the future holds.

Comparison: She can't help but compare her life to that of her peers who are either getting married or already starting families. Fear intensifies in her as she feels too late, wondering if those special seasons will ever happen for her.

JOURNEY TO CONFIDENCE

Madi began immersing herself in the Word to learn more about her fixed, positional identity in Christ. She memorized verses like Psalm 139:14 to remind herself that she is fearfully and wonderfully made by a God who has great plans for her life. She sought guidance from a seasoned member of her church who had gone through a similar season of life. That friend faithfully prayed for Madi.

Madi also realized that, in her fear, she had left little room to make herself available to meet new people. She began to make active choices that would enable her to balance her desire for career growth without ignoring her relational longing for friendship and community within her local church.

Madi began to reframe her fears into prayers of trust, and she became increasingly confident in God's provision. She no longer found herself ruminating in fear of not finding the right partner but turned these worries into petitions to God for his guidance as she surrendered to his greater plan.

CASE STUDY REFLECTION PROMPTS

1. In what way do you relate to Madi's story?

2. What could you do this week to move from fear to confidence?

SCRIPTURE FOR REFLECTION

- 2 Corinthians 5:21; 10:5
- Romans 6:1–11; 8:28
- 2 Timothy 1:7
- Isaiah 46:10

QUESTIONS FOR REFLECTION

1. In what ways do you experience fear in your longing?

2. How does the concept of a variable identity versus a fixed identity in Christ help you see your fears?

3. What part of your fixed identity in Christ encourages you the most?

4. The next time you are tempted to place your identity in anything or anyone but Christ, how will you point yourself back to truth?

5. Is there a "stage of life" question you're asked that often causes a visceral response in you? Why?

6. Was there a script that could help you prepare a response to this question?

Chapter 5

JEALOUSY & GRATITUDE

I stood on a street corner downtown, smiling for the camera in the cold while mentally calculating how many times I'd done this before. I was a bridesmaid. *Again.* That day, I would stand proudly beside a dear friend as she exchanged vows before God and loved ones. I was truly, wildly, *madly* excited for her and the groom, who had also quickly become a close friend. God was kind to grant me joy and gratitude for how he was at work. Accompanying my excitement, there was a tension settling in my gut that had become a familiar companion.

Not only was she getting married, but she would soon be moving. Our season of shared singleness was coming to an end.

On my best days, I was oohing and aahing over save the dates, planning her bachelorette party, and asking about their honeymoon plans. On my worst days, I would cry myself to sleep fighting the effects of envy in my heart. To put it simply, I was struggling with the amount of change her joy would *cost* me. *Ouch.* I was begging God to open my eyes to the gratitude I could experience over his provision for my friend.

I wasn't dating anyone at the time, so I didn't have a plus-one to bring with me to her wedding. My parents left after the ceremony, allowing me to hang out with old friends at the reception. As we transitioned to the rest of the night, the dread settled into my shoulders. *Who will I sit with? Who will I dance with? How can I make myself look like the most unbothered single person in the room?* I walked across the dance floor with a plate of food in my hand, slowly scanning for a bridesmaid who I could join so as to cut the awkwardness off at the pass. I sat down and, as the night progressed, the dance floor kicked into high gear.

I wobbled, cupid-shuffled, and cotton-eye-joed with old friends (and new!). Then, slowly and all at once, the music shifted to a slow song. I don't remember the '90s pop ballad that began billowing through the room, but I *do* remember how quickly I made my exit. Out of breath, I walked swiftly to the bathroom to give myself a minute to process.

Again, I was thrilled beyond belief for my best friend and her groom. God had written a beautiful story for them, and I was honored to be a supporting character. Deep gratitude filled my heart as I thought about the ministry team God had formed in them and all they would do together to make God known. That was *just* as true as the envy in my heart over wanting to be the one in the white gown. *Would it ever be my turn?*

It felt like I was sitting at the bottom of a cavern, looking up at a mountain. The climb would require that I actively, daily choose gratitude and surrender my selfish desires. That would be difficult, but wallowing in my sinful, selfish behavior was equally exhausting.

As the romantic ballad struck its closing chord, I sighed, nodded at myself in the mirror, dried my tears, and made an active choice to celebrate and show gratitude for how God was at work.

Jealousy clouds our view of God's provision. It is *impossible* to worship God for his goodness *and* focus our attention on what we lack. Envy is a sin struggle that accompanies longing in its unhealthier forms. At our core, we desire to be excited for others. Our thought lives often need to catch up with this desire to celebrate. This requires something that most of us struggle with: *nuance*.

God can provide the thing *we want* for someone else, *and* we can continue to trust God with our own outcome. Both can be true, but we can't deny that the balancing act of holding both can be challenging.

IT IS *IMPOSSIBLE* TO WORSHIP GOD
FOR HIS GOODNESS *AND* FOCUS OUR
ATTENTION ON WHAT WE LACK.

We must remember that our friend who got the thing we want isn't our enemy. However, the Enemy often uses such situations to distract us. The roots of jealousy can run deep and be mired with hurt and past pain. However, we can't stay there.

Let's uncover the roots so we can learn how to trust in God's timing and move forward in gratitude.

JEALOUSY'S ROOTS

Each fall, I lead a getaway for creatives, authors, podcasters, and business owners called Camp for Creatives in the Great Smoky Mountains. Fostering an environment for my peers that is free of comparison, competition, and posturing is one of the most life-giving things God has ever asked me to do, but it is no small task. It's common to go to a conference or retreat with fellow writers and speakers and instantly sniff out comparison, like a perfume the attendees didn't ask to wear in the first place, when you walk in most rooms.

When I shared with an attendee how I intended to start the getaway, she said, "Rebecca, the way you lead tonight will set the tone for the rest of the weekend."

As I stood to welcome everyone to the opening night, I shared how we were all on the same general path—seeking Jesus, making him known in our business or ministry—but almost all of us were at different stages of that journey. That's where the comparison typically begins. *Where am I compared to others?* If we focused on what OTHERS in the room were accomplishing, we would miss what God had in store for us.

"It will be tempting to compare where you are on the journey to the woman to your right or left. I just want to say that comparing, posturing, and any other way the Enemy wants to distract us this weekend has *absolutely no place* in this cabin." The conviction with which I said these words surprised me. But the statement was met with a loud roar across the room of "Yes!" and "Amen!"

What followed brought me to tears multiple times throughout the weekend. Women who were just beginning to explore their gifting by drafting their first book proposals were giving ideas to a woman who had recently been a guest on *Good Morning America*. Podcasters with hundreds of thousands of downloads were giving advice to attendees who felt called to start their own. It was a beautiful dance of giving and receiving; that's something I want to create as often as I possibly can for women in my industry.

The best part? When one of the attendees told me, "I felt like I was able to take my Spanx off this weekend!" We laughed and, in that moment, I knew I had accomplished what God had led me to do.

IF WE FOCUSED ON WHAT *OTHERS* IN THE ROOM WERE ACCOMPLISHING, WE WOULD MISS WHAT GOD HAD IN STORE FOR US.

I wonder if, in your circumstance, reading that story feels like a breath of fresh air. Does it give you hope that it's possible to experience this type of collaboration and celebration?

We have to identify where the root of our sin struggle is coming from in order to move forward. In most cases, the root of our jealousy is comparison.

The world tells us: **Someone's step forward is my step backward.**

God tells us: **God's provision, to me or someone else, is worthy of my gratitude.**

Now, while it might be difficult for us to admit it, our thought lives prove that we frequently allow the Enemy to shift our focus to the wrong place. But we can stop this vicious cycle, especially when we learn that envy is a key strategy in the Enemy's playbook.

Let's peek behind the veil for a moment. I've often noticed the following cycle in my own life when I struggle with comparison. I wonder if you can relate to this path to jealousy:

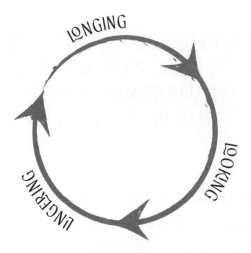

Longing: I notice something I desire. This is usually a God-given desire. Remember, just as the temptation to sin is not sin itself, the acknowledgment of a longing is not sin; rather, it is natural and good. What we *do* with the desire is what matters most.

Looking: I begin noticing others who have been given the experience I'm longing for. This is natural, and we can't (nor should we) just divert our eyes from anything that resembles the blessing we desire. This would cause us to miss many meaningful experiences in life.

Lingering: I ruminate on how I feel about another person's lived experience of what I want. When we linger, we become hyperfixated on our desire, often to the extent that it causes harm. At the very least, it causes us to take our eyes off Jesus.

Lingering is what causes us to stumble into jealousy. We can experience longing and even observe others' joy, but when our minds lock in on the disparity between their experience and ours, we step into sin.

When we allow ourselves to live in this never-ending cycle with no accountability, we are creating well-paved neural pathways that will become more natural with each twinge of envy we experience.

"How in the world do we stop it?" I understand why you'd ask. To combat jealousy, we must pre-decide to flip feelings of envy to feelings of gratitude.

As children of light (1 Thess. 5:5), God will give us opportunities to expose the darkness. Think of your response like a flashlight beaming into an otherwise dark room.

When you're tempted with jealousy, what if you intentionally chose to speak words of life over the person you're jealous of?

When you're tempted to skip the wedding or baby shower because it feels too difficult, what if you intentionally fixed your eyes on how you see God creating something beautiful?

When your friends are experiencing grandparenthood while your kids are trying to conceive, what if you celebrated how God was at work in them despite life looking different than you imagined?

What if God chooses to use each opportunity as, dare I say, an encouragement in your own journey? Scripture tells us that "death and life are in the power of the tongue" (Prov. 18:21). Speaking words of encouragement over someone will halt the cycle of jealousy and turn our hearts toward gratitude.

Allow your words of support and celebration to be an offering of worship to God. As we consider how to move toward gratitude, we must cling to this theological anchor:

God's provision, to me or someone else, is worthy of my gratitude.

God is worthy of our praise and gratitude. God is worthy of our obedient yes to having gratitude in all things (1 Thess. 5:18). Consider the following scripts that you can use when you're interrupting the cycle of jealousy and responding in faithful obedience.

- I'm reminded of the kindness and love of God in his timing for you.
- I'm praising God for his generosity in your life!
- This reminds me that God has a unique plan for each of our lives. I'm excited to watch his plan for you unfold!
- Your blessing is a testament to God's faithfulness. Watching you helps me trust in his promises for me as well.
- How can I support you?
- Your joy is sowing seeds of joy in me too!
- How can I pray specifically for you?
- You're doing a great job!
- I'm proud of you.

This week, try to find an opportunity to exercise gratitude as you see God's blessings in someone's life. It will encourage them and help you begin to normalize this as a response to your waiting. It may feel unnatural at first, but we can strengthen this muscle of gratitude over time.

DON'T TAKE IT PERSONALLY

Many years ago, I was a part of a long-standing small group. When a group meets for a long time, the dynamics eventually change, which is a beautiful part of community. When we started, apart from our leader, we were *all* single. Our leader had such a heart for the stage of life we were experiencing and specifically wanted to encourage and equip single women. Our stories matched up, our tensions felt eerily similar, and our longings sounded the same.

It was a beautiful mix of shared experiences, and we even had an older women's group graciously offer their wisdom to us once a month or so. We would invite them to our small group after submitting questions related to a number of topics (marriage, purpose, finances, and more). It was the safest community I've ever known.

As our lives continued to unfold, several group members began dating and eventually got married. To our rejoicing, God was answering our prayers, and the group morphed into a mix of single and married women. As such, new women began attending the group. It was a gift to learn about their struggles, and in turn, those of us who were still waiting to get married learned a lot about how to prepare our hearts. Hear me: I do believe effective community can be formed between married and single people. It can be complex and challenging to watch God meet someone else's longing with provision while we continue to wait; however, it is possible to handle these situations gracefully when our hearts are fixed on God.

One night, we were going around the room sharing prayer concerns with one another, and one of the newer ladies began sharing that her husband was out of town that week. She said, "I absolutely hate staying alone at night. I get really fearful, and I dread spending several nights alone. Will you pray that God will help me with my fear and keep me safe while he is away?"

Confession: *I was fuming.* How could she ask for prayer for something that was the *daily* reality of over half the room? I thought, *I will leave this room to go home, alone, as I do every night.* In the moment, my flesh kicked in, threw up a wall, and wondered if a discipleship environment with married and single women was for me anymore.

Now, was that taking things to the extreme? *Absolutely.* I had taken her genuine concern personally when it had nothing to do with me (or my singleness). When we're struggling in the cycle of longing, looking, and lingering, we can often stew on words spoken, realities insinuated, and perceived hurt that was *never* projected on us in the first place.

To take it a step further, a great temptation in moments like this is to respond in defiance and communicate why our reality is worse than theirs. I've often seen this referred to as "hardship Olympics." This kind of competition is exhausting and can create undue hurt for another person. Just as we can stop the cycle that leads us to jealousy, we also have the choice to respond in genuine concern and care for the other person as an act of worship to God.

In hindsight, I wish I would've handled the situation differently. If I had a do-over, I would've called her the next day to let her know I was praying and ask if she'd like to come over for dinner one night that week to have some girl time.

As we battle to surrender our jealousy to God and respond in gratitude, may we recognize when we've stepped over the line and repent. May we remember that someone else's hardship isn't a personal vendetta toward us, and we shouldn't take it personally.

DON'T COMPARE RESULTS

A common challenge in both vocational and relational longings is when jealousy bubbles up based on someone else's results or success. I don't have to look very far to notice instances like this in conversation and in my own lived experiences. I was recently chatting with an aspiring author and answering her questions about how to get a book published, how long it takes, and the challenges of the publishing industry.

I told her that, for me, it took nearly nine years of writing (for free!), honing my craft, building a network, discerning who I felt called to serve, and finding a literary agent before I signed on the dotted line and secured a traditional publishing contract. She was certain that God wanted her to get her message out (and FAST!), and she was willing to do anything in her power to circumvent the system and make it happen. I recognized the grit and urgency in her voice because it sounded a lot like my own a decade ago. Ready, sure, but lacking the scars of rejection, disappointment, and waiting that naturally come with the process of publishing.

There is only one way to get those scars, and it's through experience. That experience can only be gained by enduring time under tension. The more we talked, the more I realized that her vision for the speed at which she would publish revolved around comparing herself to female Christian authors who've been in the business for decades. She finally said, "You know what? I want to know how Lysa TerKeurst does it! She puts out books superfast, and I want to know her secret."

(Now: Lysa, I love you. I hope you read these words, and I can sincerely share with you how YOUR conference, She Speaks, was a catalyst that lit a fire in my belly to want to write and speak professionally. I simply would not be where I am were it not for your obedience. You pioneered this work for the women coming behind you, and I'm forever grateful.)

That said, with all due respect, I *do not* want to be Lysa TerKeurst. Nor does her barometer for success dictate mine.

I responded by saying, "I would carefully and prayerfully consider what YOUR next step is rather than trying to achieve *her* level of success overnight."

When we expect God's timing in our lives to match up with someone else's success, all we're doing is setting ourselves up for disappointment. Rather, when we are focused on the ways God is providing in our own life, and when we remain obedient to his leading, we will have grateful hearts when the fruit comes, not disappointment because our circumstances don't look like someone else's journey.

There is nothing wrong with having a big goal and praying that God would, in a way that most befits his glory and our good, provide and sustain so we are able to thrive in our calling, our relationships, or whatever area where we are experiencing longing. The mistake comes when we compare our chapter 1 to someone else's chapter 31.

To date, Lysa has written more than thirty books (no small feat!). To compare yourself to her would diminish how God is at work in *both* of your lives, bringing each of you through specific experiences in his divine timing.

Maybe you don't relate to the author example, but perhaps something feels similar in your own heart. Consider the following questions as you examine how you're struggling with jealousy:

- How long have they been doing this?
- What kind of help do they have?

- How do I see God at work in me?
- What help do I need?
- What step of obedience can I take today in the direction God is leading?

Rather than focusing outward on others' results, let's focus on where God is leading us next. We are not responsible for how our results compare to *theirs*; rather, we are to be obedient to God alone. When our eyes are fixed on Jesus (Heb. 12:2), gratitude and praise will pour out of us. He is at work on our behalf, and our job is faithfulness.

DON'T RIDE IN THE BACK

As we all know, we live in a hurry-up world filled with brokenness and sin. At every turn, we notice new challenges, frustrations, and realities that we never expected. We don't have to look very far in the Bible to see that God explicitly states that the Christ follower should embody praise and gratitude. In the Psalms, we see King David and other psalmists declare thanks for who God is and how he is at work in their struggles.

We see this command perhaps the most clearly in 1 Thessalonians 5, as Paul gives his final instructions to the church at Thessalonica: "Give thanks in all circumstances; for this is the will of God in Christ Jesus for you" (v. 18).

At times, when considering a hard truth in Scripture, it can be easy to try to find a loophole. *Surely there's a way around this that will change my tough circumstances or excuse my sinful attitude or behavior.* It's easy to go down that road as it pertains to things like selflessness, forgiveness, and surrender.

Surely we aren't called to be grateful when …
God, it's extremely hard to practice thanksgiving when …
How can I possibly praise God during THIS?

But God gives us clear instructions when it comes to gratitude. As we read earlier, Paul instructed us to give thanks in *all* circumstances. *Every* circumstance. *Every* temptation to envy. *Every* disappointment when someone else gets what we want. *Every* time all hope seems lost. *Every* time it's too late by earthly standards. Because hope is simply never lost when it's hidden in Christ.

Our circumstances should never dictate our gratitude for God's goodness. Our worshipful response to God's holiness, mercy, and grace toward us should never hinge on what we perceive he has or (more importantly) has not provided in an earthly sense. It hinges on the reality that we now experience eternal life, unending grace, and rich mercy because of the cross of Christ.

Feelings don't always catch up with facts. Think about it like the seats on a roller coaster. Having grown up about an hour from Dolly Parton's birthplace, Dollywood is the happiest place on earth to me. There, a wooden roller coaster, Thunderhead, has been hailed as *the wildest ride in the woods*. It *always* feels faster and more chaotic if you sit in the back. The front row riders can see where they're headed, but the back row gets whipped over the crest with less warning.

In the same way, when struggling with jealousy, we can sit in the front and focus on the facts while letting our emotions ride in the back row. This doesn't mean our feelings are no longer attached to us. No, they are *definitely* along for the ride. We're just not letting them lead the adventure. That would feel like whiplash! And if they're not "there"—as in we're struggling to find gratitude or see God's goodness—they will catch up in time, just as the back row of a roller coaster will eventually crest that hill.

God gives us his Word and his Spirit to teach us all truth (John 16:13–15; 17:17). Let's sit in the front row, arms stretched wide, as we trust him to lead the way forward.

"SEARCH ME, GOD!" PRAYER

As we apply the truths we've discovered about jealousy and gratitude, let's return to our "Search Me, God!" prayer as a compass to direct us. Remember that God is worthy of our gratitude as we entrust to him our temptation to compare and envy. This prayer is simply a way to repeat back to God what you're recognizing as you examine your heart.

Search me, O God, and know my heart!
Try me and know my thoughts!
And see if there be any grievous way in me,
and lead me in the way everlasting!

Consider the following questions:

Recognize my thoughts: Where am I most tempted to experience jealousy?	

Reveal my sin: Is there a sin pattern (in word or deed) that has led to this lingering in my thought life?	
Realign my attitude: Where in my life do I need to remember that God is worthy of my praise and gratitude because of his unchanging character?	
Remember God's way: What is my next step as I turn to God in gratitude?	

CASE STUDY

Now we're going to explore a case study that I hope can help you see how jealousy and gratitude could show up in your life. This time, we'll specifically consider an example of vocational longing. Whether this example captures your current season or not, my prayer is that it helps you develop empathy for people who may be facing different circumstances.

❉ MEET SHANDA

Shanda is in her late thirties, and she holds strong aspirations to excel in her career. She aims to lead a large team and eventually climb her way to the executive team. Despite her efforts, and her great reputation with her peers, she has found herself struggling with jealousy as she watches friends and colleagues achieve success at a *quicker* rate than she does.

CHALLENGES

Comparison: Shanda's longing for advancement often leads her to compare her progress to others' success. It's easy to get caught in the cycle of looking at and lingering over her peers' new roles, glamorous vacations, and higher bonuses at the end of the year. While money isn't her main motivator, she feels that her work ethic and career performance should have earned advancements with her employer.

Self-Worth: The envy she feels has begun to chip away at her self-esteem. Doubting her abilities and worthiness has led to feelings of inadequacy. This insecurity has spilled into her relationships, causing tension at work and in her day-to-day friendships.

JOURNEY TO GRATITUDE

Shanda's jealousy was not only affecting her emotional well-being; it was also hindering her spiritual growth. She knew it was robbing her of joy, and she began asking God for guidance and wisdom in her struggle. She wanted to celebrate the steps forward that she saw her coworkers taking without perceiving their progress as a personal loss.

She made it a habit to spend time in prayer, thanking God for the blessings in her life, both personal and professional. She confided about her struggle to a wise mentor who had walked through a similar situation. Her mentor prayed for Shanda and gave her wisdom on where to fix her focus when she was tempted to envy.

The more Shanda praised God and fixed her eyes on where he was leading her specifically, the less room she had to linger on thoughts of jealousy. She began pre-deciding to celebrate others' successes, knowing their gain wasn't her loss. The more she placed her identity and hope in Christ, the more her perspective continued to shift. The corporate ladder, promotions, and accolades were no longer measures of her worth.

CASE STUDY REFLECTION PROMPTS

1. In what way do you relate to Shanda's story?

2. What could you do this week to move from jealousy to gratitude?

SCRIPTURE FOR REFLECTION

- 1 Thessalonians 5:5, 18
- Proverbs 18:21

QUESTIONS FOR REFLECTION

1. In what area of your life do you struggle with jealousy? How are you protecting your thoughts so that envy doesn't consume you?

2. Can you recognize the pattern of longing, looking, and lingering in your life? Has this cycle led you to feel envy?

3. Which script resonated the most with you? How can you use it in a future conversation with someone who's experiencing the thing you want?

4. Are you "riding in the back of the roller coaster" and letting your feelings take over? What can you do to swap seats to the front so you can embrace truth and enjoy the adventure God has for you?

5. Have you ever felt anger bubble up in you as a response to someone else experiencing what you desire? Next time this happens, how will you respond differently?

Chapter 6

ISOLATION & COMMUNITY

In the church where Dustin was interviewing for lead pastor, it was standard practice for the candidate to come and preach before the congregants voted on a new pastor. The weekend of our visit, the church hosted a reception to give congregants a chance to learn more about us. Then Dustin preached on Sunday morning before the church members voted. As you would imagine, this day can be filled with all sorts of angst, excitement, and curiosity. As a family, we were discerning whether this was where God was leading us. In turn, the *church* was doing the same.

Dustin had been in ministry for more than seventeen years at that time, but this was the first lead-pastor transition he had made, and it was the first that *we* had made together as a married couple. It was, truly, our first rodeo. Although we were assured that God was leading us here, we still battled uncertainty about relocating and buying our first home in the booming East Tennessee real estate market, where bidding wars had become the norm.

We attended the reception on Saturday with the congregation, which brought a mix of questions that revealed a lot about the state of the church. Turns out you quickly learn a lot about the culture of a church when you turn its congregants loose to ask a prospective pastor (and his wife) questions. Afterward, we decided to go to one of our favorite restaurants in the area, Calhoun's. We sat down, ordered, and processed our morning together.

As we stood up to leave the restaurant, we rounded the corner toward the front door and I heard, "DUSTIN GEORGE!" A stranger (to me) quickly stood from his table with arms wide open as he headed toward my husband. After a few seconds, Dustin said, "Hey, man … Chris!" Dustin's confusion turned into a huge smile as he recognized his old friend and former colleague, a man he had not seen in years. They laughed, embraced in a bro hug, and I turned to introduce myself to his wife, Alyssa.

There followed a quick exchange of how God had moved both of our families back to East Tennessee, when Chris and Alyssa married, and the timing of our hopeful move back to our favorite side of town. They hadn't found a church home yet, so when Dustin shared that he'd be preaching in view of a call the next day, Alyssa exclaimed, "We'll be there!"

A challenge with this new opportunity was that we had no *history* with the people within the church. Maybe you've experienced this in a job transition? In Dustin's ministerial career, he had attended the church where he'd taken his first job, so he had developed a great deal of relational equity before he was ever on the payroll. Then, when he moved to Mississippi, the lead pastor at the time had served with Dustin at his previous church, so again he had a strong connection before stepping behind the pulpit.

There's a comfort that comes in having served alongside others on your staff or in your congregation. Unfortunately, the *only* people we knew at this church were the members of the search committee and their spouses.

We were encouraged that God clearly orchestrated this divine appointment with Chris and Alyssa. The next morning as we made the drive south from Maryville for the big day, I took in all the beauty of this place I called home. We passed over a bridge, and as I gazed across the lake to my right, I noticed a flock of birds flying in a perfect V. Oddly enough, they were headed in the direction of the church. I found it peculiar that these creatures could learn to fly in such an organized pattern as they traveled south.

Of course, my next move was to quickly pull out my phone and google "why do birds fly in a v." There are a few theories floating around as to why they do this. My favorite is "to conserve energy by taking advantage of the upwash vortex fields created by the wings of the birds in front."[1] Translation: The birds rely on the wind their fellow birds stir up ahead of them.

This reminded me of a story in the Bible in which Aaron and Hur held Moses's arms up when he became too weary. With their support, Israel was able to defeat Amalek in battle (Ex. 17).

The birds provided wind beneath the wings of those behind them, so they were able to endure. That's *exactly* what God granted us in our friendship with Chris and Alyssa.

It's what we're searching for, aren't we? To be surrounded by people who will support, encourage, and defend us when we are weak. When we experience longing, it's easy to isolate ourselves and feel that no one understands us. In this chapter, we'll explore isolation and turning toward community.

The world tells us: **No one knows how I feel.**

God tells us: **God desires for us to experience friendship with him and others.**

The Enemy wants to separate us from one of God's greatest blessings: community. His job is a lot simpler if no one is holding us accountable, checking in on us, asking the right questions, or expressing their concern. Community often brings with it tears, hard conversations, unmet expectations, and disagreements. It's not always comfortable to let people in, so when we're in pain, we may cling to the lie that isolation is the only way.

I wonder if one of the following statements sounds familiar to you?

- "I don't want to be judged."
- "Shame over my past disqualifies me from experiencing community."
- "It's easier to do this on my own than constantly having to watch her get what I desire."
- "I'm terrified of the vulnerability that community will require of me."
- "She hurt me in the past, so it's difficult for me to pursue community."
- "I'm too busy for community."
- "I don't actually feel that I need community to have a growing relationship with Jesus."

No matter which statement resonates with you, can we decide that, for us, community is nonnegotiable? That it's something we must prioritize?

The hurried pace of our culture causes isolation to feel more familiar than community—both with God and with other believers.

For many of us, it's natural to drift away from community toward isolation. But we can make the intentional choice to push back against culture's narrative that we can manage our longings alone.

Where there was once isolation, there is now community. Before we put our faith in Jesus, there was a separation between us and God because of sin. This isolation from the Father was caused by the fall (Gen. 3). When Jesus came to pay the price for our sins by dying on the cross, not only were our pasts redeemed, but God extended the opportunity for us to live in fellowship with him (John 14:23; 1 John 1:3). Jesus is our mediator, our go-between (1 Tim. 2:5), who provides restoration when we repent, turn from our sin, and place our faith in him. As we grow in an abiding relationship with him, our friendship with God deepens. And one day, when Jesus returns, we will have perfect fellowship with God, void of the longing and pain we experience now.

THE ENEMY WANTS TO SEPARATE US FROM ONE OF GOD'S GREATEST BLESSINGS: COMMUNITY.

In addition to friendship with God, as followers of Christ we also have the blessing of friendship within his bride, the church. The world, and many inside the church, would like to convince you that this pursuit is too difficult, laden with struggle or filled with disappointment. They aren't wrong, and I won't deny that you might experience hardship when pursuing community in the body of Christ because it is filled with broken people. However, it's a pursuit worth chasing. We're better together (Eccl. 4:9–10), and God will use even the harder situations we walk through in the church to sanctify and strengthen us.

We have so much hope for community, not only here and now in the church but in the days and centuries to come in heaven! Chris and Alyssa were sent strategically from God as a gift of grace for what hasn't been an easy season of ministry. We've become one another's sounding boards, they are a safe place for us to be *human* (any ministry couple will understand what a rarity that can be when you live in a constant fishbowl), and every time we're together all four of us revel in how God aligned our paths. In our crazy real estate market, God saw fit for us to find homes that were only a couple of miles apart. What a gift!

REMOVING THE HUMAN TOUCH

For the first four years of our marriage, Dustin and I lived in a southern Mississippi town of around twelve thousand people. Coming from the beauty of East Tennessee and finding my place in this new community as a pastor's wife during a global pandemic left me feeling like a fish out of water. The town proudly called itself "A Homeseeker's Paradise," yet it was anything but paradise for me. While the town was quaint and charming, it lacked many modern conveniences that I had grown accustomed to back in Tennessee.

For example, the grocery stores didn't offer curbside pickup services until about a year after this option had become a nationwide standard. So, for the most part, if we wanted something, we had to drive out to fetch it, and we sometimes had to travel to a neighboring town just to find basic ingredients. Don't *even* get me started about how hard it was to find oat milk! Once, a friend offered to pick up Chick-fil-A nuggets for me while she was in Jackson. The nearest location to our town was fifty miles away. Although it may sound silly, I often felt completely removed from civilization, and I craved access to the everyday conveniences I'd always known.

I give that context to say that a surprising thing happened when we moved back to Maryville, Tennessee. It was as if we'd been living in a time warp in Mississippi. The rest of the world had moved on without us. With rideshares, apps, and online orders, there seemed to be an instant solution for *every* problem imaginable … all at the press of a button.

Our lives became especially busy during this season. We bought a house, Dustin started a new job, and I was launching my first book. Like most modern consumers, I took quick advantage of the shortcuts technology offered, even as I watched the instant access create roadblocks to community.

Why ask someone to take us to the airport for an early flight when we can call an Uber?

Why take someone up on their offer to make us a meal while we're sick if we can order our favorite soup to be delivered?

Why introduce ourselves to that new person at church when getting likes on social media fills our brains with more serotonin?

COMMUNITY IS NEVER ONE-SIDED, AND IT IS NO ACCIDENT THAT GOD HAS PLACED YOU RIGHT HERE, RIGHT NOW.

At every turn, it seems, our culture has resisted the need for a human touch and connection. Community is becoming harder and harder to find as we reject social interactions in our day-to-day lives. Virtual appointments now allow us to see a doctor, attend therapy, take classes, and even meet our next boyfriend without leaving the comfort of our home. Yet, many studies suggest we're more miserable and lonelier than any generation before us.

What if we pushed back against the trend and allowed ourselves to rely on one another again?

Let's take a look at some possible ways you can invite others into your area of greatest need and support them through their struggles too:

- **Ask for prayer.** Share a prayer concern with a friend, and ask how you can pray for them. Remember, prayer is often the means God uses to accomplish his purposes.
- **Go to lunch.** It's easy to get stuck in our routines and forget to spend time with friends and family. Invite someone to join you for coffee or lunch. Share how they can support you, and ask how you can do the same for them.
- **Ask for a ride.** The next time you travel, ask for help. Sure, it's easier to take an Uber, but save yourself the money and give someone else the blessing of transporting you to the airport. Then offer to do the same for others.
- **Handwrite a note.** Maybe someone spoke a word of encouragement and you want to thank them. Perhaps

you want to step outside of your own concerns and fears to meet someone else in theirs. Handwrite a note and see how God uses your act of kindness.

- **Invite someone into your longing.** Speaking aloud to a trusted friend or mentor about your longing requires bravery. However, it is often the step forward we need to prevent us from continued rumination, frustration, and discouragement. Listening can also be a powerful act of love. Be willing to bear witness to other people's stories as you seek community.

Community is never one-sided, and it is no accident that God has placed you right here, right now. If we pay attention, we will see many opportunities to serve others, develop friendships, offer comfort, and be comforted. Shifting our focus to how he might desire to use us in the lives of others can be a powerful source of encouragement.

How might God want to use you in your community?

ACCESSIBILITY AND INTIMACY

As you've figured out by now, my dating relationship with Dustin was long-distance. We were 545 miles apart, to be exact! Because we didn't live in the same state, we didn't have the luxury of spontaneous date nights, so we would stay up until all hours of the night discussing details of the everyday experiences we were missing in each other's lives. Our time apart drew us closer together. We had very little in-person accessibility; therefore, the depth of our friendship was largely dependent on the intimacy of our long-distance communication.

When we finally married, we suddenly began spending all our time together. This was *new* for both of us, and it was a harder adjustment than we'd expected. It became easy, for the first time, to put intentional conversation on the back burner when we were tired from a long day. Idiosyncrasies also became glaringly obvious as we were now living in the same space, as they do with any couple in their first year of marriage. I often found myself missing the deep conversations that came with living hundreds of miles apart. For the first time, we had to intentionally choose to pursue deeper friendship and intimacy together.

The same choice exists in our communion with God. We have more access to God's Word than any previous generation—podcasts, apps, ebooks, audiobooks—all in addition to physical copies of the Bible. Most of us even have the luxury of owning multiple copies of God's Word, something others might consider unimaginable, especially since there are many languages that still don't have a translation of the Bible! Plus, we have access to endless study materials to aid our spiritual growth. Yet our generation is reportedly more disconnected from an abiding relationship with Jesus than any other.

Sadly, the COVID-19 pandemic had staggering effects for church attendance and Bible reading. Access has increased, and yet the numbers show us that Christians are leaving the church in droves, becoming less and less engaged with Scripture. Why? One reason is that when accessibility increases, it's common for intimacy and awe to decrease.

We must seek him with our whole hearts and ask that he give us a hunger for his presence each day. We can boldly pray for this desire, even when we don't *feel* it, because it is aligned with his will (Jer. 29:13; Heb. 11:6).

Similarly, we must seek out opportunities to build community and deepen friendships. Our capacity to do so will shift from season to season, but the first step toward building community is recognizing our need for it.

If you sense a drift toward discouragement, cynicism, or fear, it might be helpful to share your burdens with a friend and pray for each other. Be on the lookout for opportunities to be in fellowship with other believers, especially when it feels inconvenient (Eccl. 4:9–12). Chances are, that's when you need it the most!

WORLDVIEW SHIFTS

Boldly pursuing Christ is becoming more challenging by the day. As the world grows darker, it's crucial that we shine the light of Christ everywhere we go (Matt. 5:14–16). It's clear in Scripture that culture will never drift toward righteousness (Rom. 1:26–31). Instead, the world drifts toward sin, which is accompanied by a lack of accountability. A lack of accountability encourages us to walk toward sinful behavior that does not honor God.

It's become increasingly popular to alter what is considered absolute truth. From gender identity to flexible theology, we've begun to redefine what Scripture says about us as his people. As we approach conversations about our longings with others, followers of Christ or not, we will encounter a wider range of worldviews than we've ever seen. This poses a challenge as we persevere in the waiting.

I remember a time when I was single, years before I reconnected with Dustin, when a nonbelieving coworker and I got into a conversation about what I was looking for in a spouse. She began asking me questions like, "Does it really matter if he goes to church as long as he's a nice guy?" and "Would you be unwilling to give someone a chance simply because they don't share your faith?"

During the conversation, I not only felt the need to defend my convictions, but I also started to wonder if my standards were simply too high. I left the conversation thinking things like, *No man will ever be good enough*, and *The only way I'll ever find someone is if I lower my expectations*.

Perhaps you've experienced a conversation that left you feeling defensive? Or perhaps you've had to respond to someone else's disapproval?

Because of the drastic shifts in our culture, standing firm for gospel truth has never been more challenging. In that same vein, it's never been more critical that we surround ourselves with like-minded believers who can hold us accountable, point out areas where we could be settling, and direct us back to truth. It matters who we let speak into these tender matters of the heart, especially when we feel like it's *too late*.

Similarly, we will break bread, work, and even worship alongside people whose worldviews differ more broadly than ever before. This gives us reason to truly examine our hearts and know why we believe what we believe. Not only that, but we also have to distinguish between primary and secondary issues of faith.

A primary issue is a core doctrine that is crucial to understanding the fullness of the gospel. Here are examples of primary issues of the faith that God has made clear to us in Scripture.

Authority of Scripture

The entire Bible is inspired by God and "profitable for teaching, for reproof, for correction, and for training in righteousness" (2 Tim. 3:16–17). Scripture is living and active, which means God is always speaking (Isa. 55:11; Heb. 4:12).

The Trinity

God eternally exists as three persons: Father, Son, and Holy Spirit. These three (as one God) each possess fully the nature, attributes, and perfections of deity (Matt. 28:18–20; John 10:30; 2 Cor. 3:17).

Salvation

Those who repent of and turn from their sin (Rom. 6:23) and trust in Jesus Christ as their Savior become spiritually new people (2 Cor. 5:17) who are declared not guilty for their sin (Gal. 2:16) and receive the gift of eternal life. We receive salvation by grace through faith alone (Eph. 2:8–9), and it is based entirely on the death of Jesus Christ on the cross as our substitute (2 Cor. 5:14). Christ's resurrection demonstrated God's full acceptance of his death as payment for sin and foreshadows the final resurrection of all believers.

Eternal Security

Salvation grants all believers eternal life in heaven with God (John 10:27–29). Once someone accepts the gift of eternal life and experiences salvation, no one and nothing can undo or change that reality (Rom. 8:38–39; 1 John 5:13). Similarly, those who never hear, or choose to reject, the gospel will be separated from God for all eternity in a literal hell (Matt. 25:46; Rom. 6:23; 2 Thess. 1:5–12).

Gender

God created humankind, man and woman, in his image and for his glory (Gen. 1–2).

These are core, primary issues we see clearly explained in Scripture. There is no room for alternate interpretations on these matters if we uphold the authority and validity of God's Word.

There are, however, **secondary issues**—other hotly debated cultural topics—that we should approach with grace and understanding based on our interpretation of the Bible. God will guide us and give discernment through prayer and the Word (James 1:5). As we rub shoulders with others who might believe differently than we do, conversations will cause us to defend what we believe and why we believe it (evidenced by the earlier conversation with my coworker).

It's important that we ask God to reveal what would *most* glorify him in our actions. Then we can boldly and gracefully approach conversations where tension exists without hurting others, feeling like the topic is over our heads, or leaving the encounter confused and full of doubt. God is not the author of confusion. He has given us "all things that pertain to life and godliness" (2 Pet. 1:3).

As we approach conversations, especially with fellow believers, it's important that we speak the truth in love (Eph. 4:15). Let's not throw the baby out with the bathwater and forget community altogether simply because it forces our hand at tough conversations. Paul shared with the church at Ephesus that this is how a mature body is formed, but it requires a deep humility on our part. We must exercise and bear evidence of the fruit of the Spirit (Gal. 5:22–23) as we stand up for our convictions. Good theology doesn't override poor character.

The world would love to feed us a cycle that looks like this:

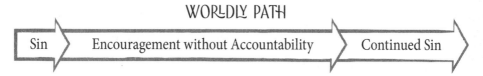

WORLDLY PATH

Sin | Encouragement without Accountability | Continued Sin

With no accountability (walking in community with fellow believers who can say hard things to us in love) we may *feel good* after others' encouragement, but we will only continue in our sinful patterns of behavior. The greatest gift someone can give us is accountability as we grow and mature in Christ. This is why God's path, which Scripture defines as a narrow road (Matt. 7:13–14), leads to the abundant life Jesus came to purchase for us on the cross (John 10:10). The cycle of life-giving friendship we are offered in biblical community looks like this:

GOD'S PATH

Sin | Accountability with Grace and Truth | Repentance | Faithful Living

What if we chose the latter? Moving from isolation to community with others requires bravery and courage. The narrow road will be paved with frustration, wondering if you got it right, and apologizing when you got it wrong, but there is joy to be found in walking step by step toward Christ *together*.

GIVING AND RECEIVING

They don't get me. I find myself thinking this a lot. In fact, it's a general sentiment I see many in my generation experiencing. In many ways, the advancement of technology has gifted (or cursed) us with the ease of So. Much. Information. More than our brains could ever begin to process! More than, dare I say, God *designed* us to process.

It's easy to feel as if you should know everything about your friend from high school and her child simply because you see glimpses of their lives online (*but what are their names again?*). Also, because we have such high expectations of ourselves in community, we often place undue expectations on others. All this pressure leaves little room for grace—for ourselves and others.

No wonder we're exhausted!

We aren't the only ones experiencing disillusionment, frustration, or discouragement in our season. Whether we're climbing a corporate ladder, awaiting adoption approval, taking a pregnancy test (again), hoping for a cured illness, seeking forgiveness for a damaged relationship, waiting on Mr. Right, anticipating a job offer, or longing for any other situation and struggling to entrust our desires to God, the experience of feeling *too late* in a *hurry-up world* is one we all share. The greatest lie we can believe is that *no one knows how we feel.*

I would answer that lie with, "Do they have to *get* it to walk in community with you?"

It's easy to compare our experience against another person's struggles. We often think:

- *They don't care because they are so focused on their own life.* This assumes the other person has ill intent toward us, which is an unfair characterization.

- *My struggles are too much for them to carry.* This is unfair to yourself because it can be a great honor to walk alongside a struggling friend.
- *Because they've not been in my shoes, they can't understand my struggle.* This leaves us as the victim of a crime the other person never committed. No one's lived experience will match ours, and we miss a blessing when we are unwilling to receive the gift of their encouragement simply because they haven't shared the same journey.

What if we truly began to see the sharing of burdens (Gal. 6:2) as a deep blessing in both directions—one to give and receive? When we're in the seat of the receiver, it will require vulnerability. When we're in the seat of the giver, it will require humility and selflessness. On the other side of that vulnerability, humility, love, and grace exists a joy that only comes by way of walking the narrow road together toward Jesus. Are you in?

NEARNESS OF JESUS

God desires our nearness. It's not that he drifts from us, but often we drift from him. In our shame, disappointment, and fatigue, it's easy to blame our *lack of a longing fulfilled* on God's seemingly deaf ear. However, don't be fooled. We must tune our ears to hear his voice and respond to his truth. As God makes the narrow path before us clearer for the next step, we must follow his lead.

Recently, Dustin and I walked through an answered prayer that ended in a different way than we had hoped. We went through all the normal stages of processing disappointment, including anger, ruminating on all the possible scenarios, and finally pressing forward in confidence of God's best. While taking a walk, I cried out to God in prayer and said, *God, you know how badly we wanted this! I don't understand why you answered in a different way than what seemed to be your best. I know you're capable, but I'm struggling to swallow the disappointment. Help me understand.*

Quietly, I sensed the Holy Spirit say, *Don't you remember that I'm working behind the scenes? I created you, I sustain you, my eye is on you, and I will provide in a way that brings me the most glory and you the most good. I care about this* much more *than even you and Dustin combined.*

All your days are numbered in his book (Ps. 139:16). He is closer than your very next breath (Acts 17:27) and desires to walk alongside you in your pain. He knows the end from the beginning (Isa. 46:10) and will work all things together for good (Rom. 8:28).

PRAYER GIVES US DIRECT ACCESS TO THE LIVING GOD, THE CREATOR OF THE UNIVERSE. YOUR FRIENDSHIP WITH HIM WILL ONLY GROW DEEPER IN THIS SEASON OF TRUSTING HIS TIMING.

Meanwhile, we get to experience a greater intimacy with him in the waiting. This requires us to listen for his voice with a greater resolve than ever before. But the nearness we feel to Jesus will directly correlate with the degree to which we are open to receiving his best, listening to his voice above all others, and following his guidance and the discernment he gives us.

You were never meant for isolation from God or his bride, the church. Before Christ, we were eternally separated from God because of sin. Jesus came to pay the full penalty of our sin and offer us the opportunity for a restored relationship and communion with God again. What grace! Jesus is our mediator. There is no longer a need for a "go-between" for God and man. Prayer gives us direct access to the living God, the Creator of the universe. Your friendship with him will only grow deeper in this season of trusting his timing.

Look to him, be honest, and receive his wisdom regarding your situation. He is near to you!

"SEARCH ME, GOD!" PRAYER

As we apply the truths we've discovered about isolation and community, let's return to our "Search Me, God!" prayer as a compass to direct us. Remember that God is near to you, and he intimately knows and grieves with you in your longing. This prayer is simply a way to repeat back to God what you're recognizing as you examine your heart.

Search me, O God, and know my heart!
Try me and know my thoughts!
And see if there be any grievous way in me,
and lead me in the way everlasting!

Consider the following questions:

Recognize my thoughts: Where am I most tempted to choose isolation, from God or others, over community?	
Reveal my sin: Is there a sin pattern (in word or deed) that has led to this choice?	
Realign my attitude: Where in my life do I need to remember that God is near to me? And that I can choose to pursue community with fellow believers?	
Remember God's way: What is my next step as I turn to God and praise him for being near to the brokenhearted?	

CASE STUDY

Now we're going to explore a case study that I hope can help you see how isolation and community could show up in your life. This time, we'll consider an example of relational longing. Whether this example captures your current season or not, my prayer is that it helps you develop empathy for people who may be facing different circumstances.

 MEET RACHEL

Rachel is in her early thirties and finds herself struggling with isolation due to painful experiences in a past friendship. The betrayal has made it challenging for her to open up and invest in community. Rachel knows the importance of finding her tribe, but she finds herself hesitant to try again, fearing more hurt and disappointment.

CHALLENGES

Pain of Betrayal: She experienced deep betrayal from a close friend, leaving her vulnerable and struggling to trust again. This broken friendship caused her to retreat and isolate as a form of self-protection.

Fear of Rejection: Her fear of being hurt prevents her from opening up to others. She fears it will lead to further rejection and emotional pain.

Vulnerability: She finds it challenging to be vulnerable with others and risk misunderstanding. This struggle has kept her from experiencing the depth of relationship she desires.

JOURNEY TO COMMUNITY

Rachel began by acknowledging her past pain and betrayal. She grieved the loss of the friendship and the trust that was broken. She chose to bring her hurt before God, seeking his healing and comfort.

She turned to Scripture and prayer for guidance on what it would look like for her to rebuild trust and find community. She took small, intentional steps toward pursuing community again by attending a new small group and investing in a new hobby (she decided to learn how to play pickleball!). Even though she sometimes felt reserved, she was *trying*.

Rachel learned that trust is built gradually as she took the time to get to know new friends and let relationship grow naturally. She recognized it was okay to move at a pace that was comfortable for her.

She worked on forgiving her past friend for her own healing and peace. She recognized that holding on to bitterness was only hurting herself and her ability to connect. Through prayer, she released the hold that the past had on her as she surrendered it to God.

CASE STUDY REFLECTION PROMPTS

1. Do you relate to Rachel's story? In what way?

2. What could you do this week to move from isolation to community?

SCRIPTURE FOR REFLECTION

- 1 John 1:3
- Hebrews 11:6
- Ecclesiastes 4:9–12
- Galatians 5:22–23; 6:2
- Psalm 139:16

QUESTIONS FOR REFLECTION

1. Where are you currently experiencing isolation? Where do you sense God prompting you to invest in community around you?

2. How have you seen culture infiltrate the way you see community?

3. How have you seen accessibility remove intimacy?

4. How could you experience the nearness of Jesus in a deeper way?

5. Where have you disregarded community because you feel that others simply don't (or can't) understand what you're walking through?

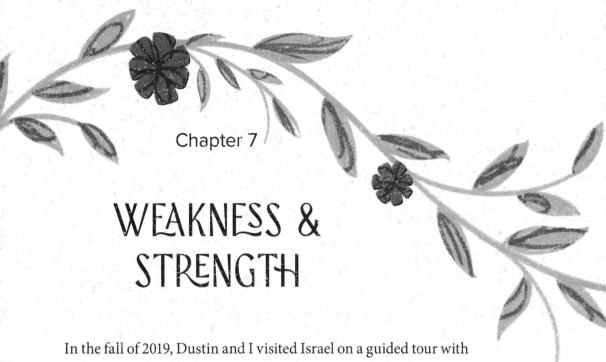

Chapter 7

WEAKNESS & STRENGTH

In the fall of 2019, Dustin and I visited Israel on a guided tour with around forty other people who longed, too, for their feet to touch the places where our Savior walked. It's not an exaggeration whatsoever to say this experience changed my life. I'll never read Scripture the same. I've often heard that visiting the Holy Land takes your Bible from black and white to technicolor. I can *confirm*!

We visited Capernaum, where Jesus taught in the synagogues; worshipped on a boat on the Sea of Galilee; baptized our fellow tourists in the Jordan River where it's believed that John the Baptist baptized Jesus; gazed at the Mount of Olives, where Jesus will return; and walked the streets of Bethlehem, the unlikely place where the Christ child was born. I have never since read a passage that references a place we went without recalling vivid memories of standing in these historic sites.

While we were there, we saw *a lot* of olives. Olives in many forms! In Capernaum, we saw an olive press as we walked through the ruins of the old town. When visiting Bethlehem, we visited an olive wood factory where we watched wildly talented artisans carve masterpieces out of wood. While standing in line to board a boat on the shore of the Sea of

Galilee, we noticed olives falling from a tree. *Tons of them.* Dustin looked at me and said, "You know, I wonder if we could grow an olive tree."

I immediately saw his wheels turning and his fingertips furiously typing questions into Google. A few minutes later, my suspicions were confirmed that he was researching what types of olive trees might grow well in Mississippi where we lived at the time.

In southern Mississippi, I could walk out of our front door wearing glasses and have steamy lenses by the time I traveled the ten steps to my car. Frequently, I'd walk out of the grocery store, put my bags in the trunk, and laugh at all the deserted shopping carts strewn about the parking lot. People gave up! It was simply too muggy and hot to survive the steps needed to return the cart. I say that because, when considering what species of olive tree would stand a chance of growing in such humidity, I knew it would have to be hearty and need very little cold weather.

It was during that research that we discovered the term *chill hours.* Chill hours represent the number of hours below a certain temperature that an olive tree needs to produce fruit. If the tree receives too many or too few chill hours, it will not bear fruit.

After learning more, Dustin said, "I think I found one. The arbequina!"

He had, indeed, discovered an olive tree that requires a low number of chill hours at temperatures below 45 degrees Fahrenheit in the winter, is low-maintenance, and is known to produce olives as early as its second year of growth.

Within weeks of returning home from Israel, the FedEx man delivered our four "baby olive trees," as we lovingly called them. (Only one ended up surviving.) Dustin cared for them for months, and eventually we decided that spending the money to purchase an arbequina that had been nurtured and cared for until it had reached five to six feet tall was worth the investment to us.

We planted it in the backyard and, over the course of a couple of years, watched it grow. We didn't miss a new leaf or area of growth! It experienced sunshine and humidity in the summer, harsh winds and rain during the storms common to our area, and quite a few *wet, cold* days of Mississippi winter. Each spring, the arbequina showed that it had thrived during our winters, just as Google told us it would.

One day, I was sitting on the back porch with a cup of coffee and a book, admiring the oasis we'd built together in the backyard, when I began to consider chill hours. Olive trees had to have them, to a certain extent, to thrive. If a species had more than its lot, it would not flower and produce fruit. In some ways, a plant's thriving depended on the weather that only God could supply.

But the opposite, amazingly, is also true. It turns out that if an olive tree, in our case the arbequina, doesn't receive *enough* chill hours, the buds on the branches won't turn into the blooms that turn into flowers and eventually bear the olive fruit. The chill, the *winter*, is what causes the tree to thrive and *produce fruit*.

I began to think about you and me and our chill hours in our seasons of waiting. Of feeling *too late* to be used by God. Winter is hard and cold and dark. We often wonder if spring will ever burst forth through the bitter cold. Apart from Christmas, I would just as soon do without winter altogether.

But what if our winters, our chill hours, are actually what cause us to thrive? What if these places where we are at the very height of our weakness help us rely completely and totally on God's strength?

Paul wrote, "But he said to me, 'My grace is sufficient for you, for my power is made perfect in weakness.' Therefore I will boast all the more gladly of my weaknesses, so that the power of Christ may rest upon me" (2 Cor. 12:9).

When we abide in the Vine, especially during our chill hours, we bear kingdom fruit. God grows and shapes us as we surrender to his ways during cold, dark moments. When we abide, we are held and kept by Jesus. May we open our frail, weak hands to the most powerful One and allow his strength to shine in our situation. We can't work our way out, hustle our way through, or manipulate our way along to spring before the sovereign hand of God wills.

When longing for fewer chill hours, remember that God sustains and strengthens you through them. He is in control. He holds all power, and he holds you in his hands. What comfort (Isa. 41:10).

SEVEN DIPS LATER

Naaman was a commander in the army of the king of Aram. He was highly regarded because, through him, the Lord had given victory to Aram. His story is nestled into the pages of 2 Kings, and we find that in addition to this victory, the disease of leprosy also marked his story.

During one of Naaman's raids across Israel's borders, he captured a young girl as a servant. The girl said, "Would that my lord were with the prophet who is in Samaria! He would cure him of his leprosy" (2 Kings 5:3).

He told the king of Aram what the young girl said, and the king offered to send a letter to the king of Israel. When the king read the letter, he tore his robes and said, "Am I God, to kill and to make alive, that this man sends word to me to cure a man of leprosy? Only consider, and see how he is seeking a quarrel with me" (v. 7).

The tearing of one's robes was a sign of deep grief and distress. The king of Israel thought that the king of Aram expected him to heal Naaman's leprosy. Knowing that was impossible, he thought he was in for a battle with the Arameans.

When Elisha heard of the king's grief, he asked the king to send Naaman to him for healing. So Naaman loaded up his horses and chariots and headed to the prophet's house. Rather than giving the directions for healing to Naaman himself, Elisha sent a messenger to the door who said, "Go and wash in the Jordan seven times, and your flesh shall be restored, and you shall be clean" (v. 10).

Naaman was angry he'd come all that way only to be told that his healing would require a massive step of faith on his part. Couldn't Elisha call on the name of the Lord and just heal him right then and there?

He suggested, in his anger, that Abana and Pharpar, rivers of Damascus, would've been much better choices to dip in than the Jordan. These rivers began in the mountains of Lebanon and flowed to Damascus. They were filled with crystal clear water that gave way to gardens and orchards. It would've been natural for Naaman to wonder why he had to dip in the Jordan as opposed to other rivers in the region. I can confirm, after being rebaptized in the Jordan, that the waters are muddy, cold, and filled with slippery silt.

But Naaman did as the prophet said and went down to the Jordan and dipped himself in the water. *One. Two. Three. Four. Five. Six. Seven.* Just as Elisha said, his skin "was restored like the flesh of a little child, and he was clean" (v. 14).

If you've never read Naaman's story, I highly recommend taking a stop by 2 Kings to read more of the context that leads up to this powerful story of healing. Something about Naaman's obedience has always stunned me. His healing, when I'm sure he felt it was too late, required continual steps of faith on his part. Steps that involved redirections, waiting, and disappointment.

Sometimes I wonder if I would've called it quits if I were in Naaman's shoes. By around the fifth dip, I bet I would doubt the last two would be worth it. Maybe there's a circumstance that feels a bit that way in your life right now.

Ultimately, it wasn't his strength that healed him. In fact, Naaman held no healing power over his disease. None of it was on him or *up to him*.

God had a bigger, grander story he was writing that would point to his strength as it intersected with Naaman's weakness. He chose to use a nasty, muddy river—one that *no one* would want to dip in once, much less seven times—as the means by which he would heal.

Our stories of longing, relational or vocational, often feel much like Naaman's probably felt. As we look at our weakness and seek to turn to God in reliance on his strength, we'll often battle against the world's lies.

The world tells us: **It's all on me.**

God tells us: **Only God is infinite in strength and capacity.**

When we realize we are hopeless and helpless apart from Christ, we can then learn to rely fully and completely on his strength. He grants us strength, courage, boldness, and discernment to take the next step of faith as he speaks to us.

God is *abundant in strength,* and his *understanding is infinite* (Ps. 147:5). The God who spoke clear instruction through the prophet Elisha to Naaman is the same God whose Holy Spirit lives in you because of Jesus' sacrifice. The same power that raised Jesus from the dead dwells inside you today (Rom. 8:11). If you're feeling weak, incapable of pressing on, or unable to see where or how God will answer your prayer, may this be an opportunity to surrender to God's greater plan.

While God is infinite and limitless in all his ways, the challenge for us is that we are *not.* Often we'll take on the mentality that we have to *do it all* by our own strength and power. Limits are a beautiful reminder that our weakness intersects with his power and ability. Longing, feeling *too late*, and wondering what the outcome will be are all incredible opportunities for us to exercise our trust in God's strength.

WEAKNESS IS MERELY AN OPPORTUNITY TO UNDERSTAND GOD'S POWER AND GOODNESS.

I have no doubt that dipping in the Jordan seven times wouldn't have been Naaman's first choice for a path toward healing. And yet, Naaman's faith to obey resulted in healing for which *only* God could have received the glory.

What in your life could only be solved by a grand display of God's strength? Weakness is merely an opportunity to understand God's power and goodness.

CONTROL THE CONTROLLABLES

I was having a *day*. You know those days when the mental, physical, and emotional load exceeds what you can bear? We were sure that God was calling us back home to Tennessee and knew the timeline would be tight. We were about two months away from the expected date when Dustin would preach in view of a call, and we were hoping to buy our first home when we moved. If you remember anything about the real estate market in 2022, you'll remember that prices sky-rocketed with no sign of them coming down—a real challenge for first-time homebuyers.

On a call with our real estate agent, I asked, "So, I've never done this before. How long will it take us to close and realistically be in a house?"

She shared a number with me, and I grabbed my calendar to do the math. The number she shared meant that to have keys in hand to a new home by the time we would travel to Tennessee for the vote, we had exactly fourteen business days to, first, find a house we could afford and, second, make an offer. Oh, and we had to (somehow) do all this remotely because we lived eight hours away (no biggie!).

Every morning, afternoon, and evening I was on Zillow scouring the available listings, overanalyzing where each house was in relation to the church and our favorite coffee shop (priorities!), and saving every dollar I could so we would be able to afford the move. It began to consume my mind, and the more I stewed, the more I realized it was utterly out of my control. There was only so much I could faithfully do in the meanwhile; the outcome truly was in God's hands.

One day, I called my mom and broke down in tears. "There is so much out of my control! There are barely any houses on the market we can afford, we need to make an offer in the next fourteen business days, and I guess we'll do all that remotely for a house we've not physically laid eyes on because there's no time for me to make a trip up there."

The dam had broken and my ability to cope with the uncertainty and weight of the situation was being tested. My desire to "fix it" was evidence of my need to trust in God and his power over the situation.

Mom kindly said, "Are you looking for someone to give advice or just to listen?" This is code for "I can tell you're upset, and I want to understand how I can help."

After listening to me swirl and ruminate, she finally said, "Sweetie, this too shall pass. In a few weeks, no matter the outcome of buying a home, you will be a resident of the state of Tennessee again. Just control the controllables."

My shoulders relaxed, I took a deep breath, and my jaw unclenched. My heart knew exactly what she meant, and the angst in my body was catching up. The entire situation, from start to finish, was an act of faith. The *only* way it was going to work out was by me completely relying on God to provide. I chose to focus on the pieces I could manage rather than swim in the anxiety of what was out of my control. In essence, I would *control the controllables.*

It is a common challenge to entrust our unknowns to God. We'll never have it together *enough*, have all the information to know how the story will end, or have enough hours in the day to manage all the tasks we need to do. However, God is always at work behind the scenes. When we are at the end of ourselves, we have the chance to open our empty hands to him and put his strength on display.

How did our story end? We closed on and took possession of a house the week after the vote. The money we had saved up for our down payment and closing costs was exactly what we needed. I'll never forget the moment I was speaking with the lender and tears streamed down my face in gratitude for how God had taken care of us.

Was it a perfect transition? Absolutely not.

Was the move all tidy, as we'd imagined? Far from it!

But God showed us his power and strength in a profound way.

CONTROL THE CONTROLLABLES, AND LEAVE THE REST IN GOD'S HANDS.

Would you allow him to do the same for you? Consider circumstances in your life that will only work themselves out by God miraculously showing up for you. Make a list of them and spend intentional time in prayer asking God to work on your behalf.

Remember, he knows your heart and is way more concerned about the outcome than you are. He is trustworthy and wise and good. He will use this season to sanctify and grow you.

Control the controllables, and leave the rest in God's hands.

"SEARCH ME, GOD!" PRAYER

As we apply the truths we've discovered about weakness and strength, let's return to our "Search Me, God!" prayer as a compass to direct us. Remember that God is at work on your behalf, and you can trust him with your heart's desires. This prayer is simply a way to repeat back to God what you're recognizing as you examine your heart.

Search me, O God, and know my heart!
Try me and know my thoughts!
And see if there be any grievous way in me,
and lead me in the way everlasting!

Consider the following questions:

Recognize my thoughts: Where am I the most challenged to ruminate on things out of my control?	
Reveal my sin: Is there a sin pattern that has caused me to believe it's *all on me*?	
Realign my attitude: Where in my life do I need to remember that God is working on my behalf? Do I believe he is trustworthy?	
Remember God's way: What is my next step as I give my weaknesses back to God and rely completely on his strength?	

CASE STUDY

Now we're going to explore a case study that I hope can help you see how weakness and strength could show up in your life. This time, we'll consider a relational longing that impacts a vocational longing. Whether this example captures your current season or not, my prayer is that it helps you develop empathy for people who may be facing different circumstances.

❀ MEET LESLIE

Leslie is in her late thirties, is married with two preschool-aged girls, and has excelled in a very demanding career in marketing. She is watching her girls grow up before her eyes and finds herself longing to spend more quality time with them. She has a long commute each workday, and the demands of her role make it challenging to achieve the work-life balance she feels her family deserves. She wants to do all things with excellence for the glory of God, but right now she feels like her family has drawn the short stick.

CHALLENGES

Demanding Career: Leslie's job demands extensive hours and high dedication, which constantly challenges her desire to prioritize family time.

Lack of Work-Life Balance: Leslie sees her girls leave day care having learned new things and reaching new milestones, and she wants to experience those things with them. She feels that she has to choose between excelling in her career and being present for her family.

Overwhelm: Leslie feels inadequate in balancing her responsibilities at work and at home. She experiences overwhelm often, with feelings of guilt both when she's at work because she misses her girls and when she's at home because she feels that she should be getting ahead at work.

JOURNEY TO RELIANCE ON GOD'S STRENGTH

Leslie began by honestly admitting her weakness to God. She prayed for continued endurance and wisdom as she acknowledged her limitations and sought his direction. She took intentional time to consider her priorities and personal values alongside her husband. Through prayer and rich conversation, she was reminded of the importance of investing as much time as possible into her girls.

Leslie sought counsel from her church family and a trusted mentor as she considered her work-life situation. She asked them to be in prayer with her as she explored what it would look like to spend more time at home. She began fully relying on God's strength to provide as she continued to navigate decisions ahead.

After much prayer, she explored flexible work arrangements and opportunities for a healthier work-life balance with her manager. She clearly communicated her desires for family time while also honoring the needs of the business, hoping to find a solution that would allow her more time with the girls.

In addition to courageously talking with her manager, she took inventory of her schedule and how she spends her time. She made intentional lifestyle changes that would create capacity to spend more quality time with her family. She began having the girls help with age-appropriate chores to lighten her load.

Ultimately, Leslie learned to lean on God's strength in her moments of weakness. Her longings persisted, but she found peace in the adjustments she was able to make. She found moments of joy in being more present with her children, realizing it was God's wisdom and presence that brought the peace her heart was yearning for all along.

CASE STUDY REFLECTION PROMPTS

1. Do you relate to Leslie's story? In what way?

2. What could you do this week to acknowledge your weakness and rely on God's strength?

SCRIPTURE FOR REFLECTION

- 2 Corinthians 12:9
- Isaiah 41:10
- 2 Kings 5
- Psalm 147:5
- Romans 8:11

QUESTIONS FOR REFLECTION

1. What unknowns are you currently facing? What would it look like to fully rely on God?

2. How do you relate to the concept of chill hours? How have the chill hours in your life produced kingdom fruit?

3. Where in your life are you striving? What would it look like to surrender your weakness as you trust in God's strength?

4. How do you relate to (or empathize with) Naaman's story in 2 Kings 5?

5. What would it look like for you to *control the controllables*?

Chapter 8

HURRY & REST

We sat at a table with small glasses of friendship tea between us. How had we forgotten the quaint, winsome experience that Apple Cake Tea Room had offered us so many times in the past? It was the place where my mom had her wedding shower and Danielle and I had shared countless lunch dates in our early years of friendship.

Danielle has been in my life for more than a decade and has seen me walk through longing, triumph, and everything in between. We were catching up as we enjoyed chicken salad, banana bread with cream cheese, and potato chips—a strange combo, I know, but it always feels like home.

Between bites, I said, "The next chapter is about hurry and rest. I'm a little nervous."

She gazed at me, eyes wide, and slowly put down her knife. "Wow. I can't wait to read it."

You see, Danielle and I are both high achievers. Every personality test I've ever taken has labeled me an achievement-driven personality. In some moments of my life, I've despised that this is how I seem to be naturally wired. In other ways, I've come to be thankful for it. I run at one speed—fast—and it requires a lot of intentionality for me to slow down, reflect, be patient, or rest.

As we were discussing this area of weakness for both of us, I reflected on the song I'd chosen for our wedding ceremony, "Love Like This" by Lauren Daigle. It perfectly describes the love of the Father *and* the love I feel toward Dustin. I especially love the way the band hushes to mezzo piano as Lauren sings "Hallelujah" during the bridge. With each passing repetition, the song begins to swell until it crescendos into the final chorus.

Every time I listened to the song leading up to our wedding, I would picture the moment when, escorted by my daddy, I would walk down the aisle toward my groom as Danielle and her husband echoed those same swelling hallelujahs.

The moment was indeed beautiful; however, I had to force myself to slow down and savor every millisecond of it.

Isn't that what we have to do in these sacred moments of longing? The lead-up, the anticipation, is anything but restful. The crescendo can't come fast enough for our hearts, but when it does arrive, we long to slow the tempo.

What if God intended the pace of our lives to look more like an agenda of *rest* than *hurry*? What if we took a deep breath, relaxed our shoulders, and allowed God to do what only he can do? We often believe the world's lie about our pace of life.

> The world tells us: **If I hurry up, the weight of my longing will decrease.**

> God tells us: **True rest only comes in God alone.**

Because we have learned that longing leads to more longing, this lie's logical conclusion will put us on a hamster wheel of achievement, running at a pace we will not be able to sustain for the long haul.

Jesus came to give us *abundant* life, or *life to the full* (John 10:10). The Enemy would love to convince us that it's easier to rush around and fill our lives with so many *good* things that we end up missing out on God's *best* for us. We can find rest and contentment in him as we wait. Rest isn't dependent on contentment in an earthly sense, but true rest is required to find contentment in God. Rest, at its core, is a *break* from the *brokenness* we experience here on earth.

WHAT IF GOD INTENDED THE PACE OF OUR LIVES TO LOOK MORE LIKE AN AGENDA OF REST THAN HURRY?

We don't have to meet everyone else's expectations (said or implied). We don't have to reward busyness and shame downtime. We must not fall for whispers from the Enemy that taunt us into believing we have to accomplish one more thing to call today a success.

We can accept God's invitation to find rest and comfort in his presence.

ALLOW YOURSELF TO BE A BEGINNER

I'd always dreamed of taking pottery classes. Like, *legit* pottery, wheel and all. Remember Alyssa, my friend from the opening of chapter 6? When we found a local studio offering Saturday classes, we signed up as quickly as possible. It was a beginner class that promised we would learn how to throw a few bowls, later coated in enamel, and collect them after a few weeks once they were fired in the kiln.

As one does, we stopped by Vienna Coffee Company (a George family favorite!) on the way to the studio to get fueled on caffeine for our time of learning. As we walked into the small, unassuming studio, slabs of wet clay sat atop tables awaiting our arrival. Then, I saw them—the *wheels*. My dream of learning how to throw pottery was finally coming true.

We put on aprons, and after some instruction we began rhythmically moving the clay on a dry surface to condition it before heading to the wheel. Everyone was given a sponge and reservoir of water to wet the clay as needed. As the term implies, we took the conditioned blob of clay and *threw* it onto the wheel. We learned it was crucial to center the clay; otherwise, it would slip off when the wheel started turning quickly (which I learned the hard way!). I also learned there was a balance in having the clay wet *enough* but not *too wet* that it began to lose its shape.

Step by step, we watched the instructor throw a *gorgeous* bowl in a matter of what seemed like seconds. Naive enough to think I'd pick up the skill quickly, I listened intently, soaking up every technique.

When she turned us loose to try it on our own, I felt confident I could do it. I threw my clay on the wheel, wet my sponge, and began forming my bowl. The first blob fell off the wheel and flung across the room within seconds, nearly hitting another classmate. *Oops.*

The instructor came and gave me some pointers on how to do better next time. I persevered through *three* more failed attempts before I finally got a blob of clay to remotely resemble a bowl (it was more of a ring dish). Meanwhile, other participants in the class were throwing bowls like they'd been making pottery for years.

I panicked. I consider myself pretty crafty, and I usually pick up things like this really quickly. What was I doing wrong?

The poor instructor continued to visit my station, patiently giving me tips on how to improve. After watching me for a minute, she noticed my heavy-handed grip on the clay and my sponge. What she didn't know was in 2020, I had begun working with polymer clay to make earrings. I'd since started an Etsy shop where I've sold hundreds of pairs of earrings, and so, unknowingly, I was putting the same amount of pressure on *this* clay that I used for polymer clay. That was the chief of my problems!

Once I began using lighter pressure, I was able to throw a really beautiful bowl (and a couple more ring dishes) by the time class drew to a close.

As we walked to Alyssa's truck and exchanged our reflections on the class, I felt regret stir in my heart. By all accounts, the class had been a great success, but I couldn't get past the notion that I had failed. Don't get me wrong, I *love* learning new things—as long as I master them quickly (facepalm!). I *despise* being a beginner.

Maybe you feel the same way about an area of longing in your life. It's possible that you're using past experience to predict future success (or failure) rather than allowing yourself the grace to just *try.*

If your longing requires that you learn (or even try!) something new, don't miss the lessons in the restful pursuit. Our hurried hearts struggle to slow down enough to savor the process of growth. When hurry is your disease, achievement is your medicine.

But what if it didn't have to be? What if we allowed ourselves to halt the hurry and find joy in the process, no matter how slow it may be?

> WE MUST NOT FALL FOR WHISPERS
> FROM THE ENEMY THAT TAUNT
> US INTO BELIEVING WE HAVE TO
> ACCOMPLISH *ONE MORE THING*
> TO CALL TODAY A SUCCESS.

PERSONALITIES OF HURRY

Hurry can take on different personalities based on the makeup of our longing. As I reflect on what stirs up hurry in me, many memories, stories, and seasons of life come to mind. I bet you could say the same. In seasons when we're awaiting something fairly certain, hurry is a natural response until we get to the finish line. We just can't wait, and every second feels like one too many!

We all have seasons when the outcome is completely out of our control, in which case hurry is a natural coping mechanism. Let's look at three different personalities of hurry, how they can show up in our lives, and how to pursue rest.

First, we all experience **joyful hurry**. Dustin and I were walking the aisles of Home Depot one day when a bag of flower bulbs caught my eye: a lily variety with black tips and bursts of orange and red on the inside. It was the type of flower that causes you to think, *Wow! There is a Creator God, and he cares about the trivial details.*

We grabbed a small bag and, after returning home, decided the bed around our mailbox was the perfect place to plant them.

In the spring, green stalks with leaves began breaking through the soil, growing tall until the blooms began to form. Once the petals began to peek through the edges of the bud, it was only a matter of hours before they would erupt with full bloom.

One day, I stopped by the mailbox to check on them as I started my daily walk.

"That one doesn't have long," Dustin quietly said as he held a bud in his hand. "It might be open by the time you finish your walk."

I laughed, but as I continued walking, I kept hoping I would return to see the flower in full bloom. My pace quickened, and my breath became a bit more labored.

Eventually, I turned back on our street, straining my eyes toward the mailbox. *There it was.* In full bloom and boastfully exposing its firecracker-and-velvet-black petals.

Isn't that joyful hurry? It's when we have confidence and assurance something will happen and, because our hearts are impatient, we quicken our pace to "get to the mailbox" as fast as we possibly can. The *anticipation of the event*, season, or dream coming true often brings more joy than the longing itself being fulfilled. The last hour of a drive to a vacation destination, the moments before walking down the aisle, and the last few days prior to giving birth are examples of moments filled with joyful hurry.

My encouragement to you during a moment of joyful hurry is to savor the wait. It will not last forever—maybe mere hours. You will pass this way but once, so don't miss what God desires to show you here. Even when the walk to the starburst lilies grows long, each step is worth relishing.

Second, we experience a **helpless hurry**. This is the hurry personality that likely compelled you to pick up this book. There is a desire in your heart that you have zero control over. You're taking next steps of faith as best you know how, but it's forcing you into complete and total dependence on God.

I was on my way home from a speaking event in Orlando, Florida, but I had an extra day to play in Disney before hopping on a plane home to Tennessee. I met a friend for coffee on Main Street in Magic Kingdom (what a dream!), rode my favorite rides, and kept an eye on the clock, knowing I'd have to leave early enough to ride the monorail, find my car, drive to the airport, and navigate security.

I left *three and a half hours* before takeoff (aren't you proud of my responsible decision?), but I began to feel concern settle in my heart when I realized I had drained my phone battery at the park. When I climbed into the rental car, I grabbed my charger and realized the aux outlet in the car was different from the type of charger I had on me. *How wonderful.* I worriedly drove to the rental car drop-off area, using the little battery life I had to navigate there.

As I pulled into the garage, the blood drained from my face when I realized that the logo for the company I rented the vehicle from was nowhere to be found. I pulled up beside a girl on the Enterprise level, and, as I explained my situation, the blood drained from her face too.

"Ma'am, I'm so sorry," she said. "The return for that company is a couple of miles outside of the airport."

"My phone is about to die, and my flight is in an hour and a half," I said with tears in my eyes, keenly aware that it was also rush hour.

She quickly explained as best she could how I would get there, and I made a U-turn to leave the garage. I stopped as I rounded the corner with around five cars ahead of me, all checking in one at a time to return their cars. *I was gridlocked. Helpless.* I actively took deep breaths, reminding myself to slow down and not drive recklessly.

As I exited the airport, I was practically yelling my prayers aloud: "God, work it out! Help me make it to the airport in time so I don't get stuck. Only you can orchestrate this!"

I pulled into the correct rental return location and returned the keys. A sweet shuttle driver must have sensed my panic because he stopped and asked how he could help. I explained the situation as he drove me back to the airport, the path now laden with 5:30 p.m. traffic.

"I will get you there as quickly as I can. I promise," he said as he made eye contact with me in the mirror.

He helped me get my luggage out of the bus, and I ran, holding suitcases on each side of me, to the security line. The scanning devices in three of the five lines were broken, and there was a sea of frustrated, tired, and anxious travelers.

I finally got through security and *sprinted* to the tram, which I rode to my gate. They were making a final call for the last couple of passengers before they closed the gate, and I made it on board just in time. "Thank you, God," I whispered as I plopped into my seat, pouring sweat from the unintentional workout.

You know the feeling. You've been *gridlocked* too (maybe you're there right now as you're reading this chapter). There is nowhere to turn but prayer in your helpless hurry.

God will meet you there. He is sovereign and holds all power to work in your situation. Ask him to show up in a way only he could be responsible for orchestrating.

A passage I often fix my heart on when I'm struggling with helpless hurry is Matthew 11:28–30: "Come to me, all who labor and are heavy laden, and I will give you rest. Take my yoke upon you, and learn from me, for I am gentle and lowly in heart, and you will find rest for your souls. For my yoke is easy, and my burden is light."

Third, we often experience **continual hurry**. Joyful and helpless hurry often lead us to assume that our lifestyle must become one of rush and anxiety. When this happens, we set our gas pedal at one speed: *fast.* We bury ourselves in busyness, always moving on to the next thing, leaving little to no time to process what's happening in our hearts or seek God. We've got it under control, and while we might say we're trusting God, our lifestyle doesn't show that we're relying on him for much of anything.

Sometimes surrender looks like resting from hurry.

We can bring our weariness to Jesus and find true rest. Constant busyness is a common way that we distract ourselves from what we'd be forced to acknowledge and feel if we slowed down long enough to cast our cares on the Lord. Turns out, hurry is a lousy coping mechanism. Real growth, goodness, and refining come from sitting at the feet of Jesus, allowing him to do a work as our weary souls find rest.

In this chapter, we're the most concerned about spiritual rest that is developed by spending time in the Word and prayer. It likely won't feel easy or natural for you to work on the practice of rest, but let's consider some ideas we could try in these moments:

- **Pray:** If you're struggling to rest, pray and ask God to help you slow your pace so you can experience his peace.

- **Journal:** Grab a journal and write down the to-do list items swirling around in your mind. Capture them in a safe place so you can let go of them and spend quality time in God's Word.

- **Read the Psalms:** When I am struggling to rest, I'll either read psalms in my analog Bible or listen to them on an audio Bible app. Need some suggestions? Start with Psalms 3; 23; 46; and 131.

- **Drink water:** Evidence supports a connection between an increase in water consumption and decreased levels of anxiety and depression.[1]

- **Practice box breathing:** If you feel anxious, and you're trying to enter into a time in the Word, take a few minutes to do some box breathing. Inhale for a slow count of four, hold your breath for a slow count of four, exhale for a count of four, and then hold for a count of four. This technique is known to enhance your mood, lower anxiety, and increase oxygenation and blood flow to the brain.[2]

Try one or more of these techniques in seasons of continual hurry to help slow your pace so you can hear from God. Next, let's look at some practical ways to structure longer periods of rest.

I'M ONLY READING FICTION

When my mind wanders to a peaceful place, I think about where Dustin and I vacation as frequently as we can. Our love for the beaches in

Florida's Emerald Coast runs deep, particularly this tiny stretch of the Emerald Coast where we've found a resort that now feels like a second home. We went for our second anniversary and haven't missed a year since. The water is crystal clear, and the white sand squeaks between our toes as we walk down the shoreline. It's quickly become our favorite place to unwind and have deep, restorative rest together.

Before marrying Dustin, I would go on a long weekend beach trip here and there with a friend, but I hadn't taken a weeklong vacation since high school. The first time Dustin and I spent seven days on the beach, I found myself incredibly restless. I scrolled social media to avoid boredom, read a bit of nonfiction to feel more productive, and walked countless miles on the sand to try to offset my poor eating habits that week.

There is nothing inherently wrong with scanning social media, reading books, or taking long walks on the beach (one of my very favorite parts of a beach vacation!), but the real issue was that when we came home from that vacation, I felt exhausted from having entertained myself all week. I had done everything I could think of to avoid the deep soul rest I could've experienced with Dustin and with the Lord.

Realizing my mistake, I made a new goal moving forward. Next time I took a vacation, I would come home rested and ready to jump back into our everyday life. I journaled a list of things I would do differently next time.

First, I would read … *a lot*. I would bring a Bible, my favorite childhood novel, a historical fiction read, and a cheesy love story. I wanted to laugh, hoped I would cry, and needed to get lost in another world for a while.

Second, I would celebrate rest for the sake of rest. If I wanted to sleep in and forgo seeing the sunrise, the extra hours were mine for the taking! If we wanted to take a nap in the middle of the afternoon, get a ninety-minute massage (just because!), or relax at the beach for hours, permission *granted*. Rest *was* to be the full agenda with no exceptions.

Third, and maybe the most difficult, there would be no technology allowed. The world would not stop spinning because my laptop was six hundred miles away, but my sanity *just* might be at risk if I didn't put some boundaries in place. I would set up autoresponses to signal that I was out of office, allowing my brain to properly disengage. With the exception of snagging some sunrise or sunset photos, I would leave my phone in the room. I would bring an old-fashioned paper notepad and pen to capture ideas I didn't want to forget.

Sounds glorious, right? Well, it *was*. The next September, Dustin and I returned to Florida with our new goals in place. We rested, walked the beach, shared great conversations, ate yummy food without feeling the need to work out, left phones in the room (and laptops at home!), slept late and took naps, and maybe the greatest victory of all ... *I read six novels*. We had traveled with one main intention: REST! And God immensely blessed our time away.

By the time we returned home, I had gained a rested heart and body, quality time with my spouse, and opportunities in my inbox that only God could've orchestrated to remind me he didn't "need" me working that week to accomplish his agenda. Now, I'm fully aware that taking a weeklong vacation might not be possible for you right now. There are still countless ways we can apply these same boundaries to our everyday lives. Our Saturday. Our afternoon off. Our Sunday when we get home from church.

I love that Jesus, in the Gospels, models what a lifestyle of Sabbath rest should look like (Mark 2:23–28). He was going through the grain-fields, and his disciples began collecting heads of grain. The Pharisees scolded them, saying their actions were unlawful on the Sabbath. Jesus gave a similar example from David's life to reinforce an important truth about rest (vv. 25–26). As we said at the top of the chapter, true rest comes from God alone. We don't earn it to keep it, we can't do anything to lose it, and we don't have to achieve anything to gain it. Jesus said in verse 27, "The Sabbath was made for man, not man for the Sabbath. So the Son of Man is lord even of the Sabbath."

The Sabbath was made for our delight to experience God on a deeper, more intimate level. We weren't made to earn the Sabbath by our good works of worldly achievement. In our modern culture, we have the bless-ing of living a lifestyle of Sabbath modeled by Jesus' example to us in the Gospels. It will look different from week to week and season to season; however, God will bless our obedience if we choose to lay down our hurry and pick up rest.

"SEARCH ME, GOD!" PRAYER

As we apply the truths we've discovered about hurry and rest, let's return to our "Search Me, God!" prayer as a compass to direct us. Remember that we get to rest in God alone as we lay down our lifestyle of hurry. This prayer is simply a way to repeat back to God what you're recogniz-ing as you examine your heart.

Search me, O God, and know my heart!
Try me and know my thoughts!
And see if there be any grievous way in me,
and lead me in the way everlasting!

Consider the following questions:

Recognize my thoughts: In what areas of my life am I tempted to have an attitude of *hurry*?	
Reveal my sin: Is there a sin pattern that has caused me to believe hurrying is necessary?	
Realign my attitude: Where in my life do I need to remember that true rest is found in God alone?	
Remember God's way: What is my next step as I surrender my hurry to God and receive his rest?	

CASE STUDY

Now we're going to explore a case study that I hope can help you see how hurry and rest could show up in your life. This time, we'll consider an example of relational longing. Whether this example captures your current season or not, my prayer is that it helps you develop empathy for people who may be facing different circumstances.

✷ MEET MARTHA

Martha is in her late fifties and recently became an empty-nester; she and her husband moved their youngest child, Shawn, into his college dorm about six weeks ago. While she had anticipated this transition, she found herself struggling more than she expected. She had a Shawn-shaped hole in her daily routine and quickly sensed an overwhelming urge to fill her life with activities that would distract her from the grief of an empty nest.

CHALLENGES

Overwhelm: Martha felt a sudden desire to fill up her calendar with activities that would allow her to avoid the reality of her new empty-nest season. Although it was nice to escape her emotions, the constant busyness left her feeling hurried and overwhelmed.

Relational Dynamics: With Shawn off at school, Martha longed to fill the emptiness of having him gone in her day-to-day life. She also began to recognize that being empty-nesters provided a different dynamic to her marriage of twenty-five years.

Uncertainty of the Future: Martha and the moms of many of Shawn's classmates were experiencing similar challenges. She wanted to figure out what God was calling her to in this season of newfound capacity.

JOURNEY TO REST

Martha recognized her new behavior pattern of filling her life with busyness and distraction. She began to pray that God would give her wisdom to confront this new hurry in this season of transition. This required Martha to rest in God's promises. She turned to Scripture to meditate on verses such as Matthew 11:28–30 in which Jesus talks about what it looks like to rest in him.

Martha began seeking support from her local church community and attending a Bible study group of women who were walking through a similar season. They were able to share challenges but also encourage and pray for one another through these new emotions.

As challenging as it felt, Martha intentionally carved time in her schedule for quiet reflection, which allowed her to process the hard emotions that came with Shawn leaving home. She even took an afternoon nap every now and then (a new rhythm she began to treasure). She grieved the change while also finding peace in God's presence. As she leaned into his plans for her, she began to embrace the joy that she was finding in her time with God and in community with other women.

CASE STUDY REFLECTION PROMPTS

1. In what way do you relate to Martha's story?

2. What could you do this week to move from hurry to rest?

SCRIPTURE FOR REFLECTION

- John 10:10
- Psalms 3; 23; 46; 131
- Mark 2:23–28
- Matthew 11:28–30

QUESTIONS FOR REFLECTION

1. Do you relate to the lie of "If I hurry up, the weight of my longing will decrease"?

2. How do you react to situations when you feel you are a beginner? What would it look like to try something new and give yourself permission to learn slowly?

3. When reading about the hurry personalities, did any of them resonate with your current season (joyful, helpless, or continual)? Next time you experience that hurry personality, how might you respond differently?

4. What might it look like for you to implement boundaries in your times of rest?

Chapter 9

REJECTION & REDIRECTION

I love watching what happens in a room full of women cheering for one another in their vocational longing. During one of the brainstorming sessions at my first offering of Camp for Creatives, I stood at the back of the room and watched a group of women belly laughing. The discussion group beside them was praying for one of the attendees who felt weary and discouraged, and a third was knee deep in a rich discussion about the topic of an attendee's forthcoming book. Not a word of comparison was on their lips. Not a hint of arrogance, pride, or envy found its way into the room.

With tears in my eyes, I whispered to my dear friend Carole: "Look ... *listen*. This is exactly what we prayed for!"

Later that night, Carole said something I'll never forget: "This is the *first* time I've felt welcome in a room full of traditionally published authors."

My heart sank. She had feared how others might perceive her choice to self-publish rather than publish her first book traditionally. Carole feared rejection, but as she moved through the weekend, she found community, prayer, genuine care, encouragement, and a focus on being faithful over any earthly measure of success.

We all intentionally chose to focus on the bigger picture. We set our eyes on what would matter in heaven rather than the fleeting desires and disappointments we encounter on earth.

What if we all did this in regular life?

Life experience can often inform our thought life in the future. Past rejection causes us to brace for impact the next time our hearts are placed in a position that felt vulnerable last time. The assumption? *This* (the hurt, betrayal, or embarrassment) is how it's always going to be. It's a foregone conclusion when we create an assumption about how others will respond. Much like the way Carole had been treated by other authors in the past, we too can develop an expectation of rejection rather than redirecting our course toward however God might intend to work in a situation. In Carole's instance, I'm blown away by how I see God at work in her ministry as she keeps her eyes laser focused on the work he has given her to do. Watching her experience genuine community and heal from past rejection is a gift for me to watch as her friend.

PAST REJECTION CAUSES US
TO BRACE FOR IMPACT THE
NEXT TIME OUR HEARTS ARE
PLACED IN A POSITION THAT
FELT VULNERABLE LAST TIME.

Maybe you have an area of life where you've experienced rejection and you're struggling to imagine it being any other way. As we consider rejection and the grip it can hold on us, I hope this chapter feels a bit like Carole's experience at Camp for Creatives. I hope you're pleasantly surprised at the clarity and confidence that comes from directing our attention to the bigger picture.

Keep your chin up, hands open, and eyes on where you sense God leading!

ONE MORE TIME

Sometimes the most upsetting part of rejection isn't the initial sting. It's realizing that we'll have to go through the process *again*, swing the bat one more time, and continue forward if we ever hope to see progress.

Perhaps you're in this situation right now or you see it coming. In these moments, we have an opportunity to turn from the closed door, the no, or the ghosted text thread and move toward a redirected path led by God alone.

I recently surveyed my community and asked how they've walked through seasons of rejection, what they've learned, and how they've seen God show up and provide for them. Every story of rejection was different, but the encouragement they offered was the same. They all recognized, in hindsight, that through the rejection God was offering them a redirected path toward his better plan.

Let's keep the following lie in mind as we reflect on past, or work through current, situations where we felt rejected.

The world tells us: **I'll never get *there* or be able to do *that*.**

God tells us: **God is omniscient and sees the whole picture.**

Rejection is a powerful tool of the Enemy. It focuses our attention on all the reasons why we aren't good enough or smart enough or talented enough to achieve our goals. Much like Satan's whisper to Eve in the garden of Eden (Gen. 3), we might walk away thinking, *Did God actually say …? Does he really intend for* me *to experience* that? *Will I ever have joy?*

Want to hear the good news? The Enemy doesn't get to have that kind of control over your mind, nor does he see the whole picture as God does.

God is the all-knowing One who is working all things together in a way that befits his glory (Rom. 8:28). The outcome might look drastically different than what we had in mind, but often in hindsight, we see the why behind how God moved.

Rejection, whether it be in an opportunity or from a person, can often feel like *me* against *them*. Scripture tells us that we do not war against flesh and blood but "against the spiritual forces of evil in the heavenly places" (Eph. 6:12). The lies that we often fall captive to are straight from the mouth of the one who wants to steal your joy, kill your hope, and destroy your confidence. But guess what? You have the mind of Christ (1 Cor. 2:16), and you can take your thoughts captive (2 Cor. 10:5) when the crushing weight of rejection tries to take you out. Fixing our eyes on a gospel-centered narrative will redirect our focus to our God who knows *all.*

Omniscience is a theological term that means God knows *everything*. Nothing escapes his attention or care, including the grief associated with your rejection. Not only does he know *about* your rejection, but Jesus himself experienced it firsthand during his earthly ministry. Isaiah 53 foretells this suffering and rejection:

> He was despised and rejected by men,
>   a man of sorrows and acquainted with grief;
> and as one from whom men hide their faces
>   he was despised, and we esteemed him not.

> Surely he has borne our griefs
>   and carried our sorrows;
> yet we esteemed him stricken,
>   smitten by God, and afflicted.
> But he was pierced for our transgressions;
>   he was crushed for our iniquities;
> upon him was the chastisement that brought us peace,
>   and with his wounds we are healed. (vv. 3–5)

The compassion of Christ is staggering when we consider the weight of our sin in light of God's righteousness and holiness. Jesus left his throne in heaven to be born of a virgin, Mary, in an unlikely backwater town called Bethlehem. During his earthly ministry, he knew he was here for one purpose: to take OUR place on the cross to pay the full penalty for our sin. He was *rejected by men*, beaten bloody, flogged mercilessly, mocked, and ultimately crucified on our behalf. He knew the bigger picture: the will of the Father was for him to atone for the sins of the world. He took our place, bore our cross, and endured pain and agony to bring us freedom from sin and eternal life free of pain and suffering.

Now, as followers of Christ, we can stand in confidence that he has a greater, bigger, better plan for our lives. It's not up to us to understand, but it's up to us to submit to and obey his direction.

GET IT TO HAVE IT

A bit of a panic can well up in us when we experience rejection in a *vocational longing*. Many jobs require that we check a certain number of boxes before we're deemed ready for the assignment. Many times, to lead or tackle a certain project, companies will want to ensure you have previous experience. For an organization, there's a risk involved in giving responsibility to an employee who doesn't have proven success. I've worked for organizations that did this well and others that did this *not* so well.

Experiencing rejection due to lack of experience can sting, particularly for someone whose personality is marked by achievement and a desire to help others. We have to *get* experience to *have* experience. It's easy to feel stuck and wonder what we can do to move forward.

When you need to get experience to move in the direction you feel God leading, consider the following ideas to help you gain forward momentum:

> **Learn independently:** What could you do to research and learn more about the area you're hoping to gain

experience in? Pick up a book, watch training videos, join a membership community, or read some online articles. As you are waiting for God's direction on how to move forward, have a learning mindset by educating yourself in areas where you don't yet have lived experience.

Ask questions: Use this time to learn from someone who *has* the experience you *want*. Go straight to the source! If you have an established relationship with the person, treat them to coffee for an informal mentoring session where you can get curious and ask questions. If that's not possible for you, consider hiring a coach who can educate you and help with your next steps.

Don't be afraid to try again: Sometimes we have swung the bat in pursuit of our desire so many times that it feels frustrating to continue trying. Don't give up! You only need to meet *one* person. It only takes *one* right opportunity to get that experience. If God has truly given you a heart for something and you feel peace about continuing in that direction, don't be afraid to try again.

God often uses time to grow us more into his likeness as we're waiting on things like a promotion, a yes, an acceptance letter, or a positive pregnancy test. There is much for us to learn in the delay. You are not too late because of the rejection you've experienced. God is likely using it to mature and grow in you something that you'll need in the future.

EMPTY CISTERNS

Our rejection will cause us to turn to something or some*where*. It's the nature of the territory. Our attention, our heart's affection, must be directed toward a new endeavor. The disappointment causes a hole in our hearts the size of whatever we didn't receive, and it leads to a crisis of choice. Where will we turn?

The prophet Jeremiah speaks about Israel forsaking the Lord (Jer. 2). He said they had committed two evils: (1) forsaking him, the fountain of living waters, and (2) hewing out cisterns for themselves that could hold no water (v. 13). These vessels, or reservoirs, would slowly gather water from the rain over time. More than likely, they were large holes dug in the bedrock. Sounds great, but sometimes after months or years of hewing out this solid stone, rains would come and fractures would begin to form in the rock. Little by little, these fractures would begin to give way to larger cracks that would prevent the cistern from holding water. The cistern had the input of the water, but just as quickly as it came *in*, it would flow *out* through the cracks.

This word *hew* means to chop or cut away something. Although we don't live in ancient Israel and don't use the word *hew* much at all in our modern language, a similar principle can be applied to our lives as we allow God to redirect us after rejection. A natural response for us might be to, figuratively speaking, find some rock and hew out our own cistern to hold water as if it's all on us.

Anything we place our hope in apart from Christ will crack and cleave under the pressures of a hurry-up world. We can misdirect our affection in many ways, including by placing a high emphasis on the opinion of others. We can't allow their approval or disapproval to dictate our future direction. Don't let those who don't support you *kill your confidence*. Don't let those who do support you *inflate your ego*.

As we allow God alone to redirect us, may our hearts cleave to him. May he be *enough* for us. May his affirmation be the only approval we need.

What are the empty cisterns in your life that he's prompting you to exchange for his better plan? He has hewn out a better cistern, one that will never run dry. He is our living water, our provider and protector. He is so very trustworthy.

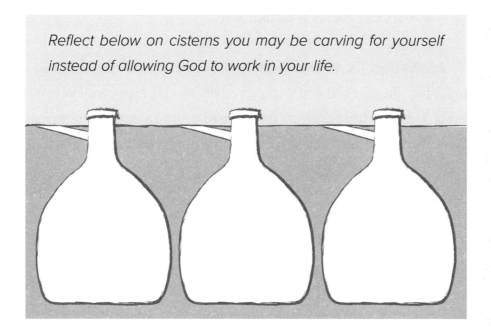

Reflect below on cisterns you may be carving for yourself instead of allowing God to work in your life.

CLOSED DOORS

A close friend to rejection is a closed door. In addition to the knowing that we'll have to *try again*, the resounding *clap* on the doorframe and

the turn of the knob can crush us. It can bring more questions than
answers. Maybe your questions sound something like the following:

> Did it have to end this way?
> What if they were wrong about me?
> Can I prove them wrong?
> Or would I prove them *right*?
> What does this mean?
> Where will I go next?
> Who else will I meet?
> Will I *ever* get to experience that?

I won't deny the validity of these questions—or the ones you'd add
to my list. They are real and visceral and often valid. However, I've come
to allow myself the chance to view a closed door as a gift of clarity from
God. When our heart rate slows, our breathing goes back to a normal
rise and fall, and our nervous system recovers from the shock, we can
make the *active* choice to look toward Jesus and say, "You know better. You know best! Thank you for this gift of clarity. Thank you for the
rescue I didn't know I needed."

We will never *drift* toward this way of thinking apart from the Holy
Spirit at work in us.

Clarity is his kindness whispering over us, "Trust me. I have a better
answer." The process of sanctification is what God will often use to hew
out a more Christlike *you* as you surrender to the process.

If you've read my work or known me for any length of time, you've
learned about my love for '90s country music. If personalities were

genres of music, *that* would be mine. When I consider how I feel on the other side of closed doors, I can't help but think of Garth Brooks's lyrics in "Unanswered Prayers." The song is a hopeful recounting of a married man running into an old high school flame at a hometown football game. He reflects upon his old desire to marry her and how he told God if he granted this wish, he'd never ask for anything else. But the man now thanks God that he didn't answer that prayer.

That sounds like many of our prayers when we experience longing, doesn't it? We feel too late and, if God could only wave a magic wand and grant us what we desire, we would leave him alone. As we know from our deep dive into the effects of longing, this simply isn't true. The longer we experience brokenness here on earth, the more *reliant on God* we must become. There is simply no other way.

His answer at times will be a closed door that takes the wind out of our sails. Although it's difficult to receive, it doesn't mean he is indifferent toward your emotions or the pain of your rejection. Rather, he's extending a gift of grace and protection that you simply couldn't have known you needed. It drives us toward a dependence on him that says, "There is nothing on earth that I desire besides you" (Ps. 73:25).

May we praise him for the closed door, trust him for the future door that will open, and wait on him when we experience confusion in the hallway.

REJECTION'S GRIP

Rejection grips us and can affect every area of our lives. Bitterness, anger, and fear of the future can seep into the deepest recesses of our hearts.

I've seen it in me. I've seen it in people I love. I especially see it in my industry, just as you likely see it in yours. It's the death by a thousand cuts that leaves us exhausted, weary, and cynical when we attempt to hope for the future.

Each of us has a long-standing history with the word *no*. Sometimes it was used for our good, like when a parent told us it was unsafe to walk across the street in oncoming traffic. Other times it was used to harm us. I wonder if any of the examples below might feel familiar.

- **Bullies:** Maybe you experienced them as a child. Name-calling, rude jokes, and discouraging words can take root in our hearts at an early age. It takes deep heart work to undo these wounds.
- **Gatekeepers:** Perhaps you're in an industry that has a group of people who "gatekeep" who gets in. Experiencing rejection from them can feel like there's a cool-kids club that you're not invited to and can cause you to doubt your calling.
- **Emotional abuse:** Maybe a parent, coach, spouse, family member, or friend in your past explicitly told you that you didn't have what it takes, made you feel unwanted, said you'll never make it, or sought to tear you down with their words.
- **Scarcity:** It's possible you've experienced the effects of rejection in other people's lives. It's common that when others experience rejection, it fuels a fire in our flesh that says, "I have to press on and work harder, no matter who I hurt or step over in the process."

If an ounce of that feels true to your past, I just want to say I'm deeply sorry. I can't make the effects of those wounds disappear, although I wish I could. If we were to sit across from each other, I would be honored to bear witness to your wounds as we offer them back to God for healing. There is no quick cure, no way to "do better" to dig our way out of the hurt, and no use pretending it doesn't exist. This is deep stuff that only God's grace can heal.

While I am far from a trained therapist or counselor, I want to offer you some encouragement. We don't have to be held captive to our wounds, and we can find freedom in Christ. Staying stuck and ruminating on past hurt only keeps us further from the healing journey we will experience when we offer our hurt to God. While we can't ignore the pain, allowing it to consume our lives gives the Enemy a stronghold. Let's consider a few ways to move forward in a Christlike way.

Repent

Ouch, I know. I wish I didn't have to start here, but the effects of our hurt are a deep heart issue we must work through with God. Despite the compounding effects of hurt, we are not given a blank check for a sinful response.

Does your response to rejection bear evidence of the fruit of the Spirit (love, joy, peace, patience, kindness, goodness, faithfulness, gentleness, and self-control)?

REPENTANCE IS HARD, HOLY WORK IN THE LIFE OF A CHRIST FOLLOWER, BUT THERE IS SUCH FREEDOM IN THE WORDS "I'M SORRY."

If not, repentance can set you free from the weight of rejection. Spend some time in prayer, confessing how your past hurt has impacted your attitude and actions. Repenting of sin doesn't discredit what happened to you. It says, "Gone are the days where this hurt has control over me. In Jesus' name!"

It's also possible that, in the process, your hurt has caused you to *hurt* others. Again, repenting of this doesn't undermine or excuse what happened to you. As you reflect, if God brings someone to mind that you need to apologize to, be quick to do so. Repentance is hard, holy work in the life of a Christ follower, but there is such freedom in the words "I'm sorry." I promise you'll feel lighter on the other side.

Forgive

In all honesty, I'd give anything for there to be a theological loophole in God's command for us to forgive. As I look across Scripture, I just don't see one. If repentance is hard, forgiveness is harder. "Be kind to one another, tenderhearted, forgiving one another, as God in Christ forgave you" (Eph. 4:32). "For if you forgive others their trespasses, your heavenly Father will also forgive you, but if you do not forgive others their trespasses, neither will your Father forgive your trespasses" (Matt. 6:14–15). The call to forgive is evident all over the pages of Scripture.

But how? Many of us struggle with forgiveness because we feel as if true forgiveness erases the impact of the initial offense. Saying the words "I forgive you" doesn't negate what happened, but it does prevent the situation from having control over your thought life any longer. There may be situations in your life where it is healthy for you to have that conversation and you may find healing in saying those words to the person. It's also just as likely that because of toxic behavior, you feel unsafe to do so. It is still possible, between you and God, for you to forgive, particularly if the person is no longer with us. Forgiveness equals freedom.

Share

Have you ever shared this hurt with a trusted friend or family member? If you are the only one who knows of this hurt, it's easy to feel like you're carrying it all by yourself. You don't have to navigate repentance and forgiveness alone. Share the situation with a safe, trusted friend. Ask them to join you in prayer as you seek your next steps.

Seek

I put this suggestion closer to the end because I'm fully aware that seeking professional help, through a therapist or counselor, is not always a financially viable option. However, many organizations and local churches offer free counseling. Don't let the *fear* or *shame* of getting help stand in the way of your freedom. It can be extremely helpful to share your hurt with someone who has a completely unbiased opinion. Again, the goal is not to "fix" what happened but to heal from the brokenness.

Live

Take a deep breath. On the other side of this challenging work, you get to be a change agent. Hurt can be one of the greatest teachers in life, making us keenly aware of how rejection feels. Pain can teach us *who we want to be when we grow up*. It gives us empathy to be able to live differently in spite of our past. May it be God's greatest gift, in disguise, as he molds us into the likeness of Jesus. As we say in the South, the buck *can* stop with you. You can't control the way other people treat you, but you *can* control how you treat other people.

"SEARCH ME, GOD!" PRAYER

As we apply the truths we've discovered about rejection and redirection, let's return to our "Search Me, God!" prayer as a compass to direct us. Remember that God can redirect our path on the other side of hurtful rejection. This prayer from Psalm 139:23–24 is simply a way to repeat back to God what you're recognizing as you examine your heart.

Search me, O God, and know my heart!
Try me and know my thoughts!
And see if there be any grievous way in me,
and lead me in the way everlasting!

Consider the following questions:

Recognize my thoughts: In what areas of my life am I allowing my past rejection and hurt to impact my future?	
Reveal my sin: Is there a sin pattern (such as anger, bitterness, or retaliation) that has developed in my heart as a result of rejection?	

Realign my attitude: Where in my life do I need to remember that God is omniscient and sees all things?	
Remember God's way: What is my next step as I allow God to redirect me on the other side of rejection?	

CASE STUDY

Now we're going to explore a case study that I hope can help you see how rejection and redirection could show up in your life. This time, we'll consider a vocational longing. Whether this example captures your current season or not, my prayer is that it helps you develop empathy for people who may be facing different circumstances.

❀ MEET JESSICA

Jessica is in her early forties and has spent nearly two decades in corporate America. She has gained a lot of fulfillment in helping others succeed, but as she reflects on her journey, she feels that in many instances she's helped others succeed at the expense of her own growth. As she thinks about instances of rejection that came along her path, she feels frustrated and ruminates on what feel like missed opportunities.

CHALLENGES

Disappointment: Jessica experienced a long series of rejections that began to trigger feelings of inadequacy. These (seeming) setbacks left her questioning her worth and purpose.

Desire for Growth: She gave her life, as a leader, to prioritizing others' success, often to the neglect of her own personal growth.

Identity Crisis: The rejection she's faced forced Jessica to confront what she believes about her identity. She grappled with what she knew was true, biblically speaking, and how to live like it was true.

JOURNEY TO REDIRECTION

Jessica began by acknowledging the pain she's experienced. In the past, she suppressed these emotions, not allowing herself to properly grieve with God and others. She also turned to her local church, seeking community from a trusted mentor. Her encouragement and prayers helped Jessica redirect her focus to her unchanging identity in Christ.

Jessica spent intentional time reflecting on her passions, strengths, and areas of growth. She began praying and asking God to reveal the vocational path he had in mind for her future. She repented of the bitterness and envy that had taken root in her heart from years of feeling like she was being held back so others could succeed. This was a fresh start, and she praised God for renewing her mind day by day.

She also began to embrace rejection as a natural part of life, understanding that God's plan might deviate from her expectations or hopes. She began to see these instances as opportunities to practice and deepen her reliance on God as she focused on her identity in him rather than external validation.

CASE STUDY REFLECTION PROMPTS

1. In what way do you relate to Jessica's story?

2. What could you do this week to move on from rejection and embrace God's redirection?

SCRIPTURE FOR REFLECTION

- Ephesians 4:32; 6:12
- 2 Corinthians 10:5
- Isaiah 53
- Matthew 6:14–15

QUESTIONS FOR REFLECTION

1. In what areas of life have you recently experienced rejection? Do you relate to the frustration of knowing you'll have to do this "one more time" to move forward?

2. Have you ever been in a situation where you had to *get* experience to *have* experience? Reflect on the frustration that brought and what you learned.

3. Read Jeremiah 2 and consider how you might rely more fully on God, our living water, as he hews out a *better* cistern for us.

4. In what way(s) do you need to seek healing from past hurt or rejection? Based on the ideas of next steps in the chapter, how are you going to move forward?

5. How have you seen God redirect you on the other side of rejection?

Chapter 10

RESENTMENT & REDEMPTION

As we near the end of our time in these pages, I want you to know your *feeling too late* is not in vain. There is real hope for you in the meanwhile.

To the naked eye, your life may not bear visible earmarks of that hope today, but your story isn't over yet. The inkwell hasn't run dry, and God is NOT done. It's possible that, even as you read this book, you're still wondering how God will write the end of the story. You're in good company because, even though you've heard about some of my greatest moments of longing, I'm still on the roller coaster of the continued *meanwhile* we all must surrender to God. Even while writing this message, I often felt too late, wondered if I had what it took, and found myself begging God to grant me the words you most need.

It's possible that as you've been reading, God has brought to mind some feelings, old hurts, or fresh wounds that need healing. It's also possible that, if unattended, these concerns of the heart will stack like books, one on top of the other, until the tower begins to tilt and fall. This is known as resentment, "a feeling of angry displeasure at something regarded as a wrong, insult, or injury."[1] When we face a string of wrongs, insults, or injuries over time, the cumulative effect can make it hard to find hope.

As you've discovered in this book, I've known hurt and held hurry as a close companion. I've felt too late. I've *been* too late in the eyes of the world. I've also known deep joy and true redemption that can only be found in Christ. Though our stories are vastly different, I want you to know a bit more of mine.

YOUR STORY ISN'T OVER YET. THE INKWELL HASN'T RUN DRY, AND GOD IS *NOT* DONE.

Remember when I hiked that beautiful trail with my friend in chapter 1? I was experiencing defeat and despair as I prayed to God about my desire for marriage (*again*) on that hike in the Smokies. When I posted that photo of me sitting on the bench to Instagram, I moved on. Monday came around, and life returned to my normal, hurried pace. I often thought about the beauty of that day and how God had met me on the trail. As it turns out, God would eventually use the bench as a means of redemption.

Years later, after Dustin and I had started dating, he called and said, "Are you sitting down? I've sent you a couple pictures, but I need to tell you a story to explain. Don't look at them yet."

He proceeded to tell me that years prior to my hike with Sara, he had gone fishing in the mountains by himself. It was raining, and he was really struggling to continue to hope that God would give him a wife.

He was exhausted, felt too late, and truly wondered if and how he would meet his spouse one day.

He hiked up one of his favorite trails and fished in the dreary rain. As he hiked back down, he stopped at a bench. He sat and prayed for his future wife as he watched the swishing and swirling of the waterfall in the distance. Standing up to leave, he stood behind the bench and thought to himself, *I'm going to take a photo of this bench in faith that one day I'll bring my wife here to show her one of the places where I contended for her in prayer.*

"Now, look at the pictures I sent," he said to me on the phone. I pulled up our text thread, and there before me were two photos of the same bench. The first was the photo of me on the hike with my friend that I'd posted online. The other was the one he'd taken many years earlier on that fishing trip. Out of all the picturesque stopping places in the Smokies, God had led both of us to the exact same place to spend time in prayer for our future spouse.

> The same *waterfall.*
> The same *bench.*
> The same *struggle.*
> The same *prayer.*
> The same *God.*

I often wonder what God was thinking as he watched us both, years apart, on that trail praying for each other. I like to think he thought, *Both of them have no* clue *what I'm about to orchestrate for them.*

That's the beautiful journey of trusting in an omniscient God, isn't it? He knows *all* and has the entire universe under his careful control, yet he cares about the most intimate, even minute, details of your life. Bringing us together would've been enough for me (no bench required). Yet God saw fit to write a story that bears evidence of his sovereign power.

And, yes, one day in mid-February 2019, Dustin and I climbed into his car to take a drive. I put two and two together for several different reasons. First, the day prior he'd disappeared to spend some time with my parents (if you know what I mean). Second, I had picked out a ring a few months earlier, and because we were living eight hours apart, it was hard to make anything much of a surprise.

It was a dreary morning, and as we made the turn that would take us to the national park, my heart started beating faster. We wound our way around the beautiful streams and gorgeous views. As our "queen" (Dolly Parton) said, "He is all around me, He's everywhere I look, and each new day is but a new page in God's coloring book."[2] I like to think she was on a drive like *this* when she penned those words.

We pulled into the all-too-familiar gravel lot, neither of us saying much. Words were unnecessary since we both knew why we were there. We walked for a while with no sound apart from water trickling in the streams to our left and gravel crunching under our feet. His hand in mine, we walked the familiar trail until we both sighed as we looked up ahead and saw a familiar bend that led to *the bench*. I sat down, and Dustin precariously knelt in front of me, careful not to slip on the wet ground. He reached into the pocket of his Filson waxed-canvas jacket, a staple in his wardrobe, and pulled out a black box. *You know the one.* He stretched out his arms, gently opened the box, and with tears in his eyes said, "Will you be my wife?"

I whispered "Yes," and he put the ring on my finger as he stood up to sit beside me. We prayed and thanked God for his gift, asked him to bless our marriage, and rejoiced in how he penned our story.

God is faithful because and in spite of your highest mountaintop and lowest valley. His presence and comfort are kind friends as we navigate disappointment and grief, just as his pleasure and joy are our companions as we carefully give him glory for a next step or an answered prayer.

I long to know *both*, don't you? I long for his kindness in the harvest and his care in the drought. Jesus said these words in Matthew 6:25–30:

> Therefore I tell you, do not be anxious about your life, what you will eat or what you will drink, nor about your body, what you will put on. Is not life more than food, and the body more than clothing? Look at the birds of the air: they neither sow nor reap nor gather into barns, and yet your heavenly Father feeds them. Are you not of more value than they? And which of you by being anxious can add a single hour to his span of life? And why are you anxious about clothing? Consider the lilies of the field, how they grow: they neither toil nor spin, yet I tell you, even Solomon in all his glory was not arrayed like one of these. But if God so clothes the grass of the field, which today is alive and tomorrow is thrown into the oven, will he not much more clothe you, O you of little faith?

We can't hustle or force our way into his favor. We can't worry our way into his provision. We can't manipulate his ways, just as we can't earn his approval. You are under his care, in his arms, and he is working on your behalf.

WHEN LIFE FEELS UNFAIR

Maybe you relate to the words used to describe resentment earlier: *wrong, insult,* and *injury.* I don't hesitate to believe that you've experienced pain that has caused you to question or doubt if God will move in the way you hope. Those feelings are valid and real and normal. God knows your heart and your desires even better than you do as it pertains to the area of life where you feel too late. If you feel like you've received the short stick one too many times, and resentment is building, consider the following lie from the world.

The world says: **God has treated me unfairly.**

God says: **God redeemed my past, present, and future by sending Jesus to die on the cross.**

The way God acts (or chooses not to) will often lead us to a greater place of dependence on him. Often, Dustin and I will say, "Even if it's a no, we'll praise God for his protection, his answer, and his provision."

A no, disappointing answer, rejection, breakup, or first date gone south *is*, in fact, provision from God. Our perspective might skew widely from his, but one day in heaven we will fully understand his ways. What a *day* that will be!

I simply can't leave you there today if you're struggling with this lie in particular. When we step back and see our resentment in light of redemption, everything changes.

This truth should radically change the way we see life here on earth. Before Christ, we were *dead* in our sins, and God, being rich in mercy, made us alive with Christ (Eph. 2:1–10). Salvation is a free gift from God that we receive by placing our faith in the finished work of redemption on the cross. Redemption is the act of being saved from sin.[3] Our *deadness* in sin required a sacrifice. Why? God's holiness and righteousness demanded it. In his great love, he sent his Son, Jesus, to earth to be our perfect sacrifice so we could be redeemed (our sins would be paid for with finality) and reconciled (brought back into a right standing with God the Father).

So why does redemption change the way we think?

When we consider the greatness of his grace toward us in extending redemption we'll never deserve, it changes the way we view *fairness*. When we consider the weight of our sin, it would've been completely *fair* and *just* for us to pay the penalty for our sin. What's *unfair*, and a bit staggering, is that God would show his great mercy toward us in sending Jesus.

Our brokenness beckons us to believe that redemption means *getting what we long for* in a hurry-up world. Our skewed perspective of temporary treasure often keeps our eyes off the great redemption offered to us in Christ. He redeemed our past shame, present failure, and future sins on the cross.

> OUR BROKENNESS BECKONS
> US TO BELIEVE THAT
> REDEMPTION MEANS *GETTING*
> *WHAT WE LONG FOR* IN
> A HURRY-UP WORLD.

Jesus chose to dwell among us with one goal in mind: your redemption and mine. When Jesus cried, "It is finished!" he bowed his head and gave up his spirit (John 19:30) as the Father orchestrated his plan for the redemption of his people. The greatest demonstration of grace and mercy the world has ever known!

By surrendering our desires to the leadership of Christ and placing our full hope and faith in the finished work of redemption on the cross, we receive the righteousness of Jesus and will experience eternal life with him in heaven when our days on earth are done. What a gift of unmerited grace!

DON'T REFRIGERATE THE MAGIC SHELL

Recently, Dustin and I went to Chris and Alyssa's home for a homemade pizza night accompanied by ice cream sundaes. Alyssa shopped for pizza toppings, and I brought all the accoutrements for the perfect ice cream sundaes, chief of which was the chocolate shell topping. As we made pizzas, I stood at the countertop and gently shook the Smucker's Magic Shell bottle. *Nothing happened.*

Chris said, "Man, have you ever refrigerated Magic Shell after opening it? Bad idea!"

We all laughed at how, because of the coconut oil in the mix, the substance would seize up quickly when exposed to cold temperatures.

"Throw it over there by the fire," Chris said as he spread pepperonis across his pizza.

Being cold myself, I sat crisscross applesauce by the warm fire and held my hands close to the flames. Both the Magic Shell bottle and I slowly began to warm up, and before I knew it, I could successfully shake the chocolate goodness to ready it for our sundaes.

After dinner, each of us grabbed a bowl and filled it to the brim with ice cream and nuts, and we meticulously drizzled Magic Shell on top. Seconds later, I gently tapped my spoon against the scoops of ice cream; they were now covered in a frozen layer of chocolate. As I ate my first few bites, I was struck by the speed and intensity with which the chocolate froze. The strawberry sauce Chris had on his sundae didn't freeze. The hot fudge sauce that we often put on sundaes doesn't freeze. The maraschino cherry juice Alyssa drizzled over hers only made the ice cream melt faster, but the Magic Shell … it froze almost *instantly*. The difference was one ingredient: coconut oil. Its presence allows for the "magic" effect because it solidifies when under 70 degrees Fahrenheit.

Isn't that resentment? Resentment, and its accompanying feelings of anger and bitterness, causes us to grow cold and indifferent toward the things of God. The only way forward is to focus our eyes on the Light as we crouch down by the fire. We knock the chill off our resentment when we fix our eyes on Jesus' redemption for us. Gratitude and resentment simply can't coexist in our hearts.

When we view our life in light of eternity, we remember how temporary our pain here on earth truly is. An expanded view of where we are headed changes the way we view our current reality.

This *is not* it, my friend. I've often heard Dustin say, "The best the world has to offer is the best that a nonbeliever will ever experience; the worst the world has to offer is the worst that a believer will ever experience. In other words, this is the best there is for those outside of a relationship with Christ, but this is as bad as it will ever be for those who know him."

As followers of Christ, we place our full hope in the reality that we have all eternity ahead of us to worship and praise God for the redemption of our souls.

SOME KIND OF GOOD

It helps us to know there's information we are not privy to and would be overwhelmed by if God granted us permission behind the curtain. We often wonder, *Could I get a director's cut to know more of what is at play behind the scenes? What is God orchestrating that I cannot see?*

If suffering and waiting and want were merely due to chance, luck, or misfortune, it would render our longing impossible to swallow. There would be no plot, no hero's journey, and no resolution to leave us with hope. There would be no meaning, just pain. However, we know that to be false after spending any time at all in Scripture.

> He called his creation good.
> He is good.

His character is good.

His ways are good.

His plan is good.

C. S. Lewis wrote,

> I do not know why there is this difference, but I am sure
> that God keeps no one waiting unless He sees that it is
> good for him to wait. When you do get into your room
> you will find that the long wait has done you some kind
> of good which you would not have had otherwise. But
> you must regard it as waiting, not as camping. You must
> keep on praying for light: and, of course, even in the
> hall, you must begin trying to obey the rules which are
> common to the whole house. And above all you must be
> asking which door is the true one; not which pleases you
> best by its paint and paneling.[4]

He keeps none of us waiting a second longer than his desire for our
sanctification requires. It is a good thing for us to sit in the hallway,
gazing at the doors before us, completely reliant on his voice for the
choosing. It is *some kind of good* for us to need hope. It is *some kind of
good* for us to crave redemption.

Proverbs 21:1 tells us, "The king's heart is a stream of water in the
hand of the LORD; he turns it wherever he will." Your life is a stream of
water in the palm of his hand. Its twists and turns are but an opportunity for him to shine mightily through your weaknesses and waiting.

> IF SUFFERING AND WAITING AND WANT WERE MERELY DUE TO CHANCE, LUCK, OR MISFORTUNE, IT WOULD RENDER OUR LONGING IMPOSSIBLE TO SWALLOW. THERE WOULD BE NO PLOT, NO HERO'S JOURNEY, AND NO RESOLUTION TO LEAVE US WITH HOPE.

In my own moment of surrender at the bench, I had no idea how God was at work behind the scenes. Theologians often use the term *meticulous sovereignty* to describe God's care and control over his creation. I didn't know on that hike that God was molding and crafting a man who would desire the same values as me in marriage. A man whose highest allegiance would be to Christ alone. A life partner who God would use to refine me and show me more of who he is.

When I first began dating Dustin, I came across a blog post where he outlined thirty ways to pray for your future wife. I've probably read it no less than 894 times. In it, he described his desire for marriage this way:

> I know I don't know all the struggles we will face in marriage or the depth I will need to die to self or the difficulties of each of us being sanded and, at times, rubbed raw by the sinfulness of the other … but I want it.
>
> I want it all.
>
> I want the joys and tears and slammed doors and making up and concerns about the future and the grace

of God's provision. I want dinners growing cold under heavy conversation and prayers offered up sweetly like incense.

I want to ponder paint swatches for the eighth time and not be able to fully grasp an appreciable difference in the exact shade for the living room walls but know that it's not about the paint or the walls but the lining of a nest and the nest is the home and that is how it should be.

I want to sit up late to rock the baby and fix the dishwasher and change the oil and take out the trash and rotate the tires and go to the store in the middle of a rainstorm to pick up products for her that a single guy never thinks about.

I want to make coffee and rub feet and bring flowers and notice her hair and leave notes and call just to say I was thinking of her.

I want sore knees and lost sleep and tear stains from praying for her.

I want dirt under my nails and grit between my teeth and my tunic flecked with my own blood from wading into battle on her behalf.

I want the tango. Stumbling and tangled and on each other's toes yet trying to find the rhythm of doing life together by the grace of God. Hearing the same notes and learning the steps and no longer two but one and being willing to step back onto the dance floor again and again.

I want to put a ring on the hand of a woman I can look at and say, "Help me become like Christ, and I will spare nothing to do the same for you."

I want holiness even through the hurt.

I want sacrifice and service and sanctification if it all kills me in the process, and I know it will; it must. Every day walked with Christ requires a cross for death to self.

I want her to look down at my hand around her hand and easily imagine nail prints.

There is no other way.[5]

The first time I read that passage, my heart ached and I thought, *Ah, that's it.* I wasn't longing for perfection, a standard no man could meet, or a fairy tale that was too good to be true. My heart longed for a partner in sanctification who would lead me closer to Christ. Someone who would walk with me through joy, pain, celebration, waiting, surprise, disappointment, regret, unmet expectations, and valleys of life.

Turns out that in our almost six years of marriage, we have pondered paint swatches (and landed on the right one—Behr's Doeskin Gray!), he's rotated my tires, we've drunk more coffee than I'd like to admit, and our wrinkle lines and additional gray hairs certainly bear evidence of sleepless nights intermingled with deep belly laughs. More importantly, there has been holiness through hurt. God has used our defeats and our triumphs to refine a Christlikeness in us that wasn't there before. I'm often reminded of a Tim Keller quote, one we had read at our wedding ceremony, in which he defined marriage:

Within this Christian vision of marriage, here's what it means to fall in love. It is to look at another person and get a glimpse of the person God is creating, and to say, "I see who God is making you, and it excites me! I want to be part of that. I want to partner with you and God in the journey you are taking to his throne. And when we get there, I will look at your magnificence and say, 'I always knew you could be like this. I got glimpses of it on earth, but now look at you!'"[6]

I want to be a part of what God is doing in Dustin George for the rest of our days. As we said in our self-authored wedding vows, we often remind each other, "I love you the most I ever have and the least I ever will." Marriage, in its purest form, is an imperfect reflection of Christ and the church (Eph. 5:25). I can't wait to be laid before God's throne, worshipping him in all his goodness, and exclaim, "I knew it! God allowed me the closest view of your sanctification and gave me small glimpses of how he was at work, but now look at you! You are like him!"

What a day that will be for all of us! Revelation 21 tells us that the first heaven and earth will pass away when God sends the new heaven and new earth, the Holy City, from heaven. God will dwell perfectly with us again in the Eden-like existence that we all long to experience. Tears? *No more.* Death? *No more.* Mourning, crying, and pain? *Never again.*

Sin won't even be a distant memory (Isa. 65:17–18). Band-Aids won't fill drugstore shelves, and boo-boos won't sting. Sore joints and chronic pain won't plague glorified bodies. Ibuprofen bottles won't rattle around in our purses, just waiting on the next pain that needs fixing.

Life insurance and 401(k)s will render themselves useless. Kleenex will go out of business, and the pharmaceutical industry will be out of luck. Cancer, breakups, wars, playground fights, paper cuts, migraines, and nerve pain will no longer be a part of our language. Prostitution, slander, murder, lying, and stealing will not pervade the perfection we long to experience. Antidepressants and antianxiety medications will cease to exist. Graveyards and funeral homes will be no more. We won't need energy drinks, and hospitals will close their doors forever. Everything we're grasping to fix, patch, mend, or heal will be made new. We won't remember *anything* but perfection, and grief will be *done*.

All our desires will ultimately be met in him, and our earthly longing will deem itself insignificant in light of the goodness of God. Let's ready ourselves here on earth as we fix our eyes on the One who will perfect all creation. This is called glorification, the ultimate perfection each follower of Christ yearns for on that final day when we either take our last breath or Jesus comes back for his own.

This day is not that day but, in the words of worship artist Cory Asbury, "The story isn't over, if the story isn't good."[7]

Either here on earth or one day in glory, you will experience the perfection of God's plan for your story. If the story isn't good, keep offering it back to him in surrender as you await God's plan for your redemption. As the prophet Zephaniah exclaims, "The LORD your God is in your midst, a mighty one who will save; he will rejoice over you with gladness; he will quiet you by his love; he will exult over you with loud singing" (Zeph. 3:17).

If you feel too late in a hurry-up world, may you extend your arms in worship and pray something I've often heard Dustin pray as we trust in God's timing:

God, I trust you. If what I am praying for is too little, do whatever will bring you the most glory.

This is not the end, and *you* are not too late.

"SEARCH ME, GOD!" PRAYER

As we apply the truths we've discovered about resentment and redemption, let's return to our "Search Me, God!" prayer as a compass to direct us. Remember that God is writing a bigger story than we can comprehend here on earth. This prayer is simply a way to repeat back to God what you're recognizing as you examine your heart.

Search me, O God, and know my heart!
Try me and know my thoughts!
And see if there be any grievous way in me,
and lead me in the way everlasting!

Consider the following questions:

| **Recognize my thoughts:** In what areas of my life am I allowing resentment to build? How can I fix my eyes on the redemption offered to me in Christ? | |

Reveal my sin: Is there a sin pattern I need to repent of that has allowed resentment to grow in my heart?	
Realign my attitude: Where in my life do I need to have an eternal perspective of my longing?	
Remember God's way: What is my next step as I allow God to redeem my story and guide me?	

CASE STUDY

Now we're going to explore a case study that I hope can help you see how resentment and redemption could show up in your life. This time, we'll consider a relational longing. Whether this example captures your current season or not, my prayer is that it helps you develop empathy for people who may be facing different circumstances.

❋ MEET MEGAN

Megan is in her thirties, and she finds herself struggling with deep resentment over how her life has taken turns she never would have imagined. While she is newly married, something she begged God to provide for her, she's finding that marriage is a lot harder than she expected. She's struggling to fix her eyes on the greater story of redemption God is writing as she navigates the challenges of her season.

CHALLENGES

Unmet Expectations: Megan is learning that marriage is full of compromise, and she's often experiencing unmet expectations. This causes disappointment and resentment to grow. She longs for a deep intimacy with God and her husband.

Envy: She often compares her life to those around her who are thriving in their own marriages. This sends her deeper into discouragement.

Questioning God: Megan struggles to reconcile her resentment with how God is at work in her through the struggles in her marriage. She has a head knowledge that God has a plan beyond her understanding, but she often finds herself doubting his goodness.

JOURNEY TO REDEMPTION

Megan began by acknowledging to her husband that she desires a deeper intimacy with him and God. She recognized that these feelings of resentment have built in her heart and have hindered her ability to trust God's greater plan for her marriage. Megan and her husband began reading Scripture each day and praying together, asking God for his comfort, wisdom, and direction.

She also began to bravely confront the pain she's experienced in things not turning out the way she hoped by this time in her life. She has a desire for children but wants her marriage and relationship with Jesus to be a solid foundation she can stand on when she enters into motherhood. She grieved these desires as she asked God to meet her in the middle of her longing.

Megan made a conscious decision to trust that God will, indeed, be at work on her behalf. She knows there is a greater purpose beyond her doubts and questions, and that he will work all things together for her good. She surrendered her timing and expectations to his careful control and care. She knows there is a bigger picture that only God can see.

CASE STUDY REFLECTION PROMPTS

1. In what way do you relate to Megan's story?

2. What could you do this week to move from resentment to redemption?

SCRIPTURE FOR REFLECTION

- Matthew 6:25–30
- Ephesians 2:1–10
- John 19:30
- Revelation 21
- Proverbs 21:1

QUESTIONS FOR REFLECTION

1. Where are you experiencing resentment? What step do you need to take to surrender this hurt or insult to God?

2. How does the redemption we experience because of Jesus help you see disappointment from an eternal perspective?

3. Where do you need to sit by the fire, allowing God's presence to warm you and melt away any sin patterns that prohibit you from seeing how he is at work?

4. How does remembering God will ultimately redeem all creation encourage you in the waiting?

5. How have you seen God redeem your story?

LETTER TO THE READER

Hey, Friend,

Recently, Dustin and I were admiring our town as the cold temperatures slowly melted into spring. It was a long winter, and my personality was defrosting as the sunshine warmed my face. As the first tulips burst open, and our drift rosebushes showed new growth, I was filled with the hope of new beginnings and brimming with possibility. Isn't that what spring does? There's something about it that can make us stand a little taller as we hope toward the future.

As we drove through a familiar neighborhood, Dustin pointed out some trees that were completely barren. Neighboring trees were filled with green leaves and blooms, but in the center of a stranger's lawn, a wide and spreading tree waited for spring's arrival. He said, "That one's a little late to the party, isn't it?"

I giggled and said, "I think so."

We slowly passed by, and a lump formed in my throat. *That's a little bit how I feel too.*

The next day, I walked my frequently trodden route in our neighborhood and thought about the tree from the day before. As I began to notice blooms bursting open in flower beds and redbud trees staking their claim across the horizon, I also couldn't help but notice the barren trees that still lacked leaves and buds. They were anything but weak, standing fortified and tall. *They just need some time*, I thought.

Longing makes us feel too late in a hurry-up world; however, just because our leaves have yet to burst forth doesn't mean God is not at work. Sometimes the greatest work happens in the dark. The pace God intends for you will not always match the world's and will scarcely make sense to others. *That is okay.* More than that, it's *good* because it requires you to depend on God more fully than you ever have.

I pray you feel lighter after reading these pages. Longing will accompany our seasons of doubt, sneak up on us as we feel a pang of envy, surprise us when we confront our idols, and cause us to slow down as we embrace a lifestyle of rest. This is not easy work; in fact, how we navigate our waiting will largely be determined by the degree to which we are continually in awe of our Creator. Our eyes can't be fixed *anywhere* else or on *anyone* else. Lesser things will only distract us from the focus that Christlikeness demands.

His plan is *good*.

His character is *unchanging*.

His Word is *living* and *active*.

His Spirit is *within* you.

His timing is *right*.

His perspective is *perfect*.

As our time together draws to a close, I encourage you to come back to our "Search Me, God!" prayer as often as you need. I find myself doing a mental roll call as I examine my heart throughout the day.

Search me, O God, and know my heart!
Try me and know my thoughts!
And see if there be any grievous way in me,
and lead me in the way everlasting!

May we always turn back to him when our hearts wander. May we always seek his presence as our source of comfort, joy, and peace. May we experience the nearness of Jesus to the extent that anything *lesser* seems insignificant in light of his glorious grace. May we never forget the redemption we experienced because of Christ's sufferings and the eternal life we are granted as a result of the empty tomb. Now in part, but one day in full.

I am reminded of Paul's words in Philippians 1:23, "I am hard pressed between the two. My desire is to depart and be with Christ, for that is far better." We are hard pressed, but one day we will be free of longing, pain, suffering, and want. What a day that will be!

Rebecca George

ACKNOWLEDGMENTS

This message was harder (and easier) to write than my first book. Harder because longing is a heavyweight topic, and easier because it is so universal to our experience in a fallen world. Many voices spoke into this message, more than I can say in a few thank-yous.

Here's my imperfect attempt:

God, I am in awe of your trustworthiness. You are the *only* reason this book is redemptive. I praise you for the story you've written for me and glory in the unfinished pages that you'll write one day. I give them all to you as I hand over the paper and pen filled with wet ink.

Dustin, turn to the dedication at the beginning of the book. I love you!

Mom and Dad, you've championed me as I've imperfectly entrusted my longing to God. You have reminded me, *This, too, shall pass.* You have never made me feel shame when my story didn't match up with cultural expectations because you were too busy being my loudest cheerleaders (even when I felt too late).

Danielle, you saw the need for this message in its infant form. Thank you for listening to me stew and process over copious amounts of friendship tea at Apple Cake Tea Room and black bear lattes at Vienna Coffee Co. You've walked alongside me in my longing for thirteen years. I hope we have a *million* more. When I think of you, I think of the kindness of God. You are the best friend every gal dreams of, and I'll never get over God's grace to me in giving me *you*.

Susan McPherson, thank you for your excitement about this message as I nervously twirled mac 'n' cheese around on my fork at Puckett's in Franklin that night and imperfectly tried to articulate what God was revealing to me. Thanks for giving me the chance to write a message so many women desperately need.

Julie, I am so thankful for your voice and how you spoke into this project. You are any author's dream editor, and this book is stronger because of your eye. What a gift to me!

Blythe, thank you for your leadership and encouragement in my writing journey. You took a chance on me a few years ago, and because of your yes, I've had the opportunity to live out a lifelong dream. I don't take that lightly.

Writing friends and the Camp for Creatives community (you know who you are), your support and generosity fueled me as I ferociously wrote these words. You held my arms up, and I pray that holding these pages in your hands feels like a kingdom win for all of us.

NOTES

Chapter 2: Idolatry & Surrender

1. Elisabeth Elliot, *A Lamp for My Feet: The Bible's Light for Daily Living* (Ann Arbor, MI: Servant Publications, 1987), 96.

2. C. S. Lewis, *Mere Christianity* (New York: HarperOne, 2001), 136–37.

Chapter 3: Doubt & Hope

1. Maverick City Music, "God Will Work It Out," featuring Israel Houghton and Mav City Gospel Choir, track 10 on *Jubilee: Juneteenth Edition*, Tribl Records, 2021.

2. Elisabeth Elliot, *Secure in the Everlasting Arms: Trusting the God Who Never Leaves Your Side* (Grand Rapids, MI: Revell, 2020), 189, italics in original.

Chapter 4: Fear & Confidence

1. Geron Davis, "Holy Ground," Meadowgreen Music Company and Songchannel Music, 1983.

Chapter 6: Isolation & Community

1. "Why Do Migratory Birds Fly in a V-Formation?," *Scientific American*, October 1, 2007, www.scientificamerican.com/article/why-do-migratory-birds-fl.

Chapter 8: Hurry & Rest

1. Fahimeh Haghighatdoost et al., "Drinking Plain Water Is Associated with Decreased Risk of Depression and Anxiety in Adults: Results from a Large Cross-Sectional Study," *World Journal of Psychiatry* 8, no. 3 (September 20, 2018): 88–96, www.ncbi.nlm.nih.gov/pmc/articles/PMC6147771.

2. Melis Yilmaz Balban et al., "Brief Structured Respiration Practices Enhance Mood and Reduce Physiological Arousal," *Cell Reports Medicine* 4, no. 1 (January 17, 2023): www.ncbi.nlm.nih.gov/pmc/articles/PMC9873947.

Chapter 10: Resentment & Redemption

1. *Merriam-Webster*, s.v. "resentment," accessed July 13, 2024, www.merriam-webster.com/dictionary/resentment.

2. Dolly Parton, "God's Coloring Book," track B3 on *Here You Come Again*, RCA Victor, 1977.

3. Anthony Chute, "What Is Redemption? The Important Meaning for Christians from the Bible," Crosswalk, updated November 3, 2023, www.crosswalk.com/faith/spiritual-life/what-is-redemption.html.

4. C. S. Lewis, *Mere Christianity* (New York: HarperOne, 2001), xv–xvi.

5. Dustin George, "How to Pray for Your Future Wife—Part 1," *Dustin George* (blog), October 10, 2014, www.dustincgeorge.com/2014/10/10/520.

6. Timothy Keller, *The Meaning of Marriage: Facing the Complexities of Commitment with the Wisdom of God* (New York: Penguin, 2016), 132.

7. Ethan Hulse, Benjamin William Hastings, and Cory Asbury, "The Father's House," track 10 on Cory Asbury, *To Love a Fool*, Bethel Music, 2020.

PURSUE THE THINGS GOD CALLED YOU TO DO

REBECCA GEORGE

AN INTERACTIVE BOOK WITH SIX SESSIONS OF VIDEO INCLUDED

DO THE THING

GOSPEL-CENTERED GOALS, GUMPTION, AND GRACE FOR THE GO-GETTER GIRL

FOREWORD BY MICHELLE MYERS

DO THE THING

GEORGE

Perfectly blending storytelling, encouragement, and biblical insight, *Do the Thing* beckons you to pursue the passions that stir your soul. On this journey, you will discover how to:

- See your gifts and talents from a gospel-centered perspective.
- Prioritize goals related to your calling as you move forward with gumption and grace.
- Maximize your passions in the work you do every day.
- Actively partner with God to serve Him and love others.
- Overcome negative thought patterns so you can brainstorm, develop, and create with the confidence of a go-getter girl!

Today is the day to take a brave step in a purposeful direction, using God's Word as your compass to do the thing He has designed for you to do. After all, if not now ... when?

estherpress

Available at Esther Press
and anywhere books are sold

DAVID C COOK®

JOIN US.
SPREAD THE GOSPEL.
CHANGE THE WORLD.

We believe in equipping the local church with Christ-centered resources that empower believers, even in the most challenging places on earth.

We trust that God is *always* at work, in the power of Jesus and the presence of the Holy Spirit, inviting people into relationship with Him.

We are committed to spreading the gospel throughout the world—across villages, cities, and nations. We trust that the Word of God will transform lives and communities by bringing light to the darkness.

As a global ministry with a 150-year legacy, David C Cook is dedicated to this mission. Each time you purchase a resource or donate, you're supporting a ministry—helping spread the gospel, disciple believers, and raise up leaders in some of the world's most underserved regions.

Your support fuels this mission.
Your partnership sends the gospel where it's needed most.

Discover more. Be the difference.
Visit DavidCCook.org/Donate